Let

Love

Find

You

Volume One

Have You Heard God Calling?

Tom Carpenter

When forgiveness ends the need to judge, when conflict and condemnation both have gone away, there is a stillness that fills my mind. For me this is the Peace of God. When I am here all the world is here with me and I recognize this is the goal that I have sought, no matter how it may have looked. It is the single purpose for my learning, the very function of our lives. For it is here—filled by this stillness, I finally feel at home.

Introduction

The (hopefully) inspirational sayings here are collected from the past several years of my postings on our Facebook page:
Facebook.com/theforgivenessnetwork
and our Forgiveness Movement web site:
theforgivenessmovement.org/blog

It is my intention that each writing be taken as a "thought starter" for you to open your mind to new possibilities.. There is no order or sequence intended.

Sharing an idea is what gives it strength. I am hopeful these ideas of loving will help to bring us together. It Is also my hope they will serve to bring comfort and assurance when doubt arises and an encouragement for us to accept the truth about ourselves, regardless of how beautiful that may be.

It is our belief that we have sinned, become separated from God and lost His Love. Of ourselves, we do not know how to find It again. But God's Love is like creation's "magnet," drawing everything into itself. If we but open our willingness to have it, it will find us, for being part of God we are Love's Home.

Copyright 2016 Tom Carpenter
First Printing 2019

ISBN: 9781081191597
Contact: tom.carpenter@earthlink.net

For Linda, my sweetest heart,
My dearest love, my forever partner and best friend,
Whose love finally found me.

&

For Geoffrey Canavan who insisted this book needed to be
written

&

For John Winnes and Robert Holden.
Tom Hatcher and Tom Golinski
Dear and inspiring teachers and brothers

&

For Josh Atkinson and Tom Giske, whose considerable skills
mechanically made this book possible

&

For all our "kids," grandkids and great grands
Who are going to change the world

&

Especially
With all possible gratitude
for our Brother
Who patiently shows us the way Home.

Foreword
By Robert Holden

Finding Tom Carpenter was the answer to a prayer.

I had finished reading A Course in Miracles I'd waded my way through the six hundred and twenty two pages of the Text, and completed the 365 daily lessons in the Workbook. "Dear God, what now?" I prayed. "This course is a beginning, not an end," began the Epilogue to the Workbook. "You do not walk alone."

Three days later, I received a small package from a friend in New York. It was a white cassette tape, 90 minutes in length, with a homemade printed label, published by Carpenter Press. It was a recording of a talk by Tom Carpenter. The title was something like "Dialogue with Jesus." Diane's hand-written note read, "Sacred pearls of wisdom. Listen to this. You'll love it. Love, Diane." Later that morning, I sat down to listen to a little bit of Tom's talk. What I heard changed my life.

Most uncharacteristically, I phoned Tom, introduced myself, and invited him and his wife, Linda, to England to give a series of public talks. Diane had given me his number. I was newly married. I had no money. I'd never hosted a speaker before. Diane had told me Tom and Linda were flying from their home in Kauai to New York for a conference on A Course in Miracles. "London is very close to New York," I told Tom. He thanked me for my kind offer. "I'll get back to you," he said. I took that as a "No."

I got to Heathrow Terminal 2 just in time for the scheduled arrival of the 10am United Airlines flight from New York. The Arrivals board said that Tom and Linda's flight had landed already. I made a mad dash through the concourse of busy travelers. I saw Tom and Linda sitting together with their luggage piled onto a trolley next to them. As I approached we recognized and greeted each other as long lost friends reunited.

Tom Carpenter has been my mentor and friend for the last twenty-five years or so. By my calculation, we've spent at least 18 months lodging in each other's homes in Kauai, Seattle,

Oxford and London. We've presented many gatherings together. We've made a film, *Dialogue on Awakening,* produced by filmmaker Elmer Postle. My book *Holy Shift! 365 Meditations from A Course in Miracles* is dedicated to Tom, and Tom's book *The Miracle of Real Forgiveness* is dedicated to me.

Tom and Linda had moved to Kauai from Genesee, in the foothills of Denver, Colorado in 1985. Linda had always followed her interest in spirituality. And it was there she discovered *A Course In Miracles* in 1977. "Linda led the way. It was her interest in the Course that eventually drew me in," says Tom.

Tom was raised in Indiana. His family was not religious. He rarely attended church. He never read the bible. He built a successful, business building affordable homes for low-income families. There was nothing overtly spiritual or mystical about Tom's life. That said, Tom had a friend, Jimmy, who showed up occasionally in his life. "I loved Jimmy," Tom told me. "He was a spiritual seeker who talked to me about spiritual matters, like astral travel. I trusted him. I enjoyed listening to him, and I had no reason to doubt him

During a particularly tough period in Tom's life, struggling to run his business and be present for his new family, he, most uncharacteristically, prayed to God one night, asking for help. The next morning Jimmy showed up unexpectedly. They talked a while, and then Jimmy told Tom, "The real reason I'm here is because last night you chose to become a seeker and I've been asked to bring this book to get you started." He then gave Tom a copy of *The Urantia Book*, which became daily reading for both Tom and Linda. They had been instructed to focus on the section that chronicles the life of Jesus. This was when Tom first began to feel the love of God in his life.

On Kauai, Linda soon found like-minded friends who shared her spiritual interests. She hosted regular gatherings on *A Course in Miracles* at their home. Tom attended these gatherings, but freely admits he wouldn't have initiated them by himself. He participated quietly, not saying much, but he realized that the Course was offering a profound teaching on love. And, like others at the gatherings, he was struggling to understand it.

One day after one such meeting, while planting flowers Tom asked the Holy Spirit for help, though not even sure if such a spirit existed. As he explains it he offered to "make a deal" with the Holy Spirit; if He would help him understand more clearly the messages of Jesus in *A Course in Miracles*, he would be willing to share this understanding with the others. Within days Tom became aware that every question that entered his mind came with an answer.

All the messages in *Let Love Find You* are designed to assist you in becoming more spontaneously available to the love of God. I encourage you to use the words you read to go beyond the words and enter into the presence of Love that is your Divine Nature. This is what Jesus is teaching Tom to do, and this is what Tom has been teaching me to do. "Your being is the knowledge of creation," states *A Course in Miracles*.

Initially, Tom felt more comfortable referring to the Voice he heard as Brother, not Jesus. Tom was fully convinced of the identity of the Voice, but he struggled to feel worthy. The Voice told Tom, "You can call me Brother, but we'll also move toward your feeling equally comfortable in calling me "Self." (Spelled with a capital "S", the I AM God Self.)

I am so grateful to Tom for writing this book, finally! I've been asking for a long time! *Letting Love Find You* is a beautiful collection of love notes, which are daily invitations to sit with the Christ Mind and tune in to the presence of Love. This Love (with a capital "L") belongs to the Self (with a capital "S"). Allow the words you read to open your mind to Love's Presence so that love can find you. And, most of all, to be the presence of Love itself. This is how we heal our lives, how we experience miracles, and how we can help the world be a more loving place.

Robert Holden
Author of *Loveability: How to Love & Be Loved.*
London, November 2017

Preface

Everything that exists—all of creation—is an experience of thought that happens in the same one and only Mind - the Mind of God, of Creation. That is the only Mind there is. This is where we are indivisibly joined. This is where we recognize we are when our belief is free of guilt. Ask to be shown this "place" to experience real freedom, even for a moment. Feel the Love of God as it constantly embraces and sustains all that is here. Feel the recognition that this is where we all live when we abandon the idea of separateness. Now capture this moment and ask your God Self to bring it to you when you are next tempted to judge a story where conflict and suffering seem so real.

forgiveness

abandons separateness and becomes
OUR DOORWAY TO LOVE AND TRUTH

PLEASE NOTE: You will find the *f* symbol spread

throughout to remind us that forgiveness is the intended motivation and outcome for all our seeking.

Let Love Find You

We are either dreaming or awake; slaves to our perception or one with our God Self. There is no other state of mind in between. All dreams come from thoughts of separation and have no true meaning because it is not possible to divide the Mind of God where all Creation began and will eternally remain. But as you ask for and begin to feel the Love of God move through you, you recognize that there is nothing that Love did not create, those we think of as saint and "sinner" alike. There is one Love from the same Source, connecting *everything* to its Self, leaving nothing to exist outside; nothing to "live" apart from It's Loving.

The ego's perception cannot find this awareness because it has made a world to hide from the images of the sinful self it dreams can live outside the world of loving. But, in Truth, only dreams and illusions can exist apart from Love. And what has extended Love from Itself would not abandon It to dreams. There is within the dream, a different dream we call "awakening." It is still a dream because God's Presence does not sleep, but here we learn to surrender our perception of sin to a Knowing of what Love Is. We ask for and receive awareness of the Truth and begin to let this dream arise from loving choices that lead to joining.

It isn't easy choosing to live your dream by standards most of those around you seem not to accept. But ask yourself what it is you really want. Is it to pursue a world of pain and hate? Or take a chance that there is something more; to trust the feeling that comes when you reach out to someone suffering and alone, loving them in their disbelief they can be loved.

It is my hope you can let the passages you find here open your awareness to the "real" you now hiding in the image of a separate body. It is my belief that we are already everything we have ever longed and searched for. And as we open our one Mind together, joined in a single intent, we will recognize our One Self, so long denied. Then, Love being what It Is, will find you.

The Adventure Of Loving

We have made this world from thoughts of sin and so its purpose must be to illustrate that there is something terribly wrong with us. We strive to eke out a little happiness, but pain and suffering and despair are the "just rewards" we have assigned to sin. It is what we expect from the world while unaware it is our own creation, having only the meaning we give it. When the pain becomes too great, thinking that this world is where we actually are, we also look here for healing and for peace. But disappointment and more despair are what we find, for there is no real or lasting peace in a "place" whose purpose is to foster pain.

After lifetimes of frustration we now have come to learn there is no lasting peace except the Peace of God, and that is within us now. We then learn forgiveness is the key to accessing this awareness, its goal to realize that sin is impossible because it does not exist in the Awareness of God and therefore does not exist at all. There is nothing real to forgive. The world we have condemned and allowed to condemn us lives only in our thoughts, our story of sin and separation. Learning all this, and how to change it, is the adventure of loving,

Time is not real. We now but follow a path in our imagination we have taken many times before; "re-living" a moment   Cont'd

9

The Adventure Of Loving (Cont'd)

long since past. As Jesus tells us, it is a "journey without distance from a place we never left." We are in Heaven *now*, yet cannot see beyond the thought of hell we call a world.

And when the belief in sin is gone and the need for separation has passed away, the cloud that has seemed to hide the Light and Love of God will vanish as if it had never been there at all.

We can change the purpose of our world. No longer need it be a place where egos come to suffer sin's rewards. Forgive that thought and see the Face of Christ emerge where only bodies were before. It is our thoughts that make the world and it will serve the purpose that we give it. Have faith now that we are not surrendering into some new unchartered place, letting go of the only identity that we know. "Where" we go has been our home for all eternity. "Who" we will remember that we are when the need to separate from God is gone, is Who we have always been. The only surprise will be that the dream has seemed so real. Another discovery in the adventure of loving.

Listen . . . Do you hear God calling, asking for your help? It may sound like a brother asking to be loved. Someone perhaps wearing the terrorist garb, or a cloak of sickness. Or a child wanting to be reassured. We have many opportunities to hear Him call, if we are still a moment and just listen. Make this the purpose of your world, to hear Him call and offer you the gift to see and bless His holy Child that He created one with you. To love each one without a thought of what his dream is that we condemned before. Bless each one until you have blessed us all. The world will be lighter when you hear God call.

Be still and listen . . . Can you hear Him now?

There Is No Sin

ACIM (WB 101) tells us *"God's Will for me is perfect happiness,"* that this is so because *there is no sin.* To see how you feel about this, say to yourself, *"my will for me is perfect happiness. There is no sin."* Then, *"my will for the 'terrorist' is perfect happiness. There is no sin."* You must include both these statements because, in truth, they are the same statement. There is no sin. There is a fearful, guilty dream based on the single idea that sin is real. But, in God's Mind there is no sin. God's Voice speaks to us within the dream and invites us to hear this truth.

Forgive the thoughts and acts you see within the dream that *all* arise from our belief that sin is real. Awaken to the reality that God is only Love, pure Love. And so we must be the same for there is no sin in the God that created us like Himself. We can change the world, but only if we change the belief from which we made it. There is no sin. And without a cause there is no hate, no fear or sickness. There is no death. When you are tempted to justify anger because of what you see in the world, remember it is only there because you believe that sin is real. Affirm what you believe is true by forgiving every thought of "sin" you think or see. Let every former call for judgment become a call for love, because *there is no sin.*

There is No Sin

There is an exercise I find very helpful to remind me, "There is no sin." I sit quietly and let the thoughts of all those past and present that I hold responsible for inflicting pain and suffering on the world come to me. As each name appears I say, "_____, my will for you is perfect happiness because there is no sin." I feel the connection of my thoughts with theirs and say, "Let us forgive ourselves and come together, bringing peace to all the world. There is no sin." Each time I do this I find the remnants of my own unforgiveness, my resistance to giving up the belief that sin is real. Doing this also helps me in situations where I had previously "automatically" judged someone. I catch myself more quickly now and think of these as opportunities to more fully accept, there is no sin. The belief in sin is strong. It is the cornerstone of our perception of separateness. It is the cause of all our wars and suffering, our earthquakes and hurricanes. It is the reason we deprive ourselves of everlasting Love. But together, through forgiveness, we can change this belief because, in truth, there really is no sin.

The Adventure Of Loving

I am amazed at how much time I spend affirming what is *not* true about me, most of which has likely done the opposite, affirming these untrue things to be real and true. I am not a body. Nor am I the character in my story. All of this is true and necessary to understand. But I also feel the need to *positively* remind myself of what *is* true. I remember now Brother saying,

"Where you are in the process of loving who you are determines your ability to recognize the truth of yourself."

He tells us we are the very Presence of God's Love; the "Light" of the world. I feel the phrase arise, *"I am the adventure of loving."* It continues, "I am spirit. I am peace and light. I am life. *I am the adventure of loving."* It feels good. If it also feels good and truthful to you, please join me.

We are life and *life is the adventure of loving.*

The journey to Truth is as far as the distance we keep between us.

Share Your Happiness With God

The next time you are feeling happy go to the God Self and share your happiness. Invite the voice for God to "speak" to you. Open your mind to the joy of that communion. Notice how easy it is to feel Love's Presence when there is no need to deny it. Make this a habit; make being in Love's Presence the natural place to be. Now when a need for help arises and fear seems to isolate you, finding the comfort of this place and the guidance it offers you will not seem such a difficult thing to do. And, you will find your happy times, when consciously shared with God, continue to grow and gain in happiness.

Who We Are

Who we are is what the God Self Is. We don't stop being this when we lose our focus and behave like an ego. What we lose is our *awareness* of who we are. But we should keep in mind God's Awareness of us hasn't changed. His Plan for us continues to unfold perfectly. We only get in the way when we think we have failed our "shoulds." We are changing our thinking which is the cause of our habits of doing. We have not left our Father's Mind. We have not stopped being His Own Thought. This is the Vision the God Self holds. In accepting this from Him we welcome Him into our awareness and let Him change our mind.

Instantly Love Everyone You See

Feel for a moment what it would be like to instantly love everyone you see, or even think of. Imagine every moment filled with happiness, without fear of moments past or those to come. There is no sickness or conflict in the world you then see, nothing is missing in your life or left undone. This is your mindset when the thought of sin no longer distorts your thoughts or the direction they take. And who does have charge of your thoughts? Is it this thing called "ego" that seems to independently appear with ideas you would rather disown? Truth is, deep down we know it still feels better to *learn* of our holiness than simply to accept it. There still seems a distance between Love and What It has made; between what really is true and what we are just trying to accept. Our Teacher has said we can learn to accept what is true by giving love and feeling the love we receive in return. When we actually see our brother's sinlessness and feel the love that frees us both from our imagined guilt, we know the lie that sin has bound us to. And by withdrawing our judgment of him we have freed ourselves as well. Seeing holiness now where sin had seemed to be is the practice of "seeing differently." It is how we learn to see with eyes that want to love.

Proof You Are Alive

It is not the body that offers proof you are alive. It is your willingness to love, for it was love that made you like itself. It is not the body that sustains you in the world. It is your willingness to love. Nor is it your body that can experience love. It is your minds willingness to be loved. The body plays no part in who you are, but you could not exist without love. So you can stop searching for who you are. You are the Presence of Love.

The strength of our resistance to letting go of our perception – even to minimally changing it – can be seen in our determination to believe we are a body.

Judgment

Each time you are tempted to judge someone for anything, say, "I am sinless." Mean it and watch the need to judge go away.

The belief that I need to change myself is testament to whom I really believe created me.

One Mind, One Life

There is only the Mind of God where all of Life exists. This is where you live. This is where your story of the world is told from. Here there is only the harmony of peace and of joy. Here there is only Love. Outside this Mind there is nothing, but if you deny that what is here should be yours, there will seem another "place" for you to be. Truth is not threatened so neither judges nor denies your denial, for it knows that nothing will change. We can let go of this world, the one we have made, by surrendering what we thought it could offer to replace what we once had. Decide you want peace more than judgment, joy more than fear and love more than hate. In the absence of guilt it is clear this is what we *now* have. Accept this Gift God has given and bring a miracle of healing to everyone.

Without The Thought Of Sin

Think for a moment what it would be like to go about your day with your mind filled only with happy and loving thoughts. Everyone you meet has a smile and a glow of happiness about them. There is no sickness, no hunger, no conflict or lack; no striving, no blame, no expectations, no time and no death. Peace has replaced fear everywhere in this world. There is no word to describe hate for all the reasons not to love are gone. This is our state of mind without the thought of sin. This is our world when there is no guilt to judge.

f

Love Is Never Lost

To avoid feeling there is a loss of loving relationships when you leave the physical world behind, remember that Love is who you are and so must be present wherever you are! You will never feel alone when you give or receive love.

forgiveness will be an intellectual concept when used to overlook the egos behavior. It becomes a profound tool for healing when you hear your Voice for Truth whisper: "It only happened in your story; a dream impossible to be true.

In The Absence Of Guilt Love Will Arise

It is our belief we are guilty projected onto others that has created our sense of separation. To have an "object" to punish for our guilt we have made the image of a body to substitute for our real, infinite self. It is only to fulfill this purpose that the body suffers pain and dies. Forgiveness is God's Plan to end this cycle of lies. As we forgive our brother, his guilt and ours goes away. With guilt gone, the purpose of the body can be changed. Suffering and death are no longer needed to support our new self-image. Be determined to see everyone sinless. In the absence of guilt love will arise and we will see a different world. Together we will do this!

In a forgiving world pain and death are no more; and the harmony and peace of Oneness again prevail.

What Is Real?

Forgiveness acknowledges that what God did not create is not real and does not exist in "His World," but only in the stories we dream about. It is so very tempting, when my story shows me a struggling, suffering character, to ask what to do to fix what is wrong with him. When I witness the travails of the fleeing refugees or the heartbreak of those involved with a mass shooting, my thoughts want to go to what will solve their problems, how to punish those who could commit such heinous acts. How "natural" it is to immediately presume that what you see has occurred because of some "evil" person "out there." We all would be victims if this guilty world we see was real; God and the Son He created would be lost.

But if the world is a state of mind and what I see is a projection of my misperceived belief that there is something wrong with me, then changing this world must begin with changing my thoughts about me, and you. If I want to see a sinless world I must see it through my own sinlessness. If I want to offer others healing and recognition of what is true, I must first accept the truth of myself. If I want to be truly loving I must recognize that I am wholly loved.

Finding Your Loving Self

Recently someone said to me, "Don't you think it's a bit ambitious, this project to change the world?" And I said, "It would be if I had to change the world, but all I really have to change is what I want it to be." Let the magnitude of this thought really sink in: Nothing outside our mind is forcing us to hate, to suffer nor to die. We can have another world. We can choose to let go of what we have valued in the past. We are loved, we want to love and the very Presence of Love is everywhere in our one Mind, waiting only to be recognized and accepted. We have now been given the means and the support to change our mind. Through our use of forgiveness, we can reshape our thinking, creating a habit of looking for what is "right" about each other, and finding our loving Self in the bargain.

forgiveness ends the need to learn for now
you know that you are free to love.

forgiveness asks only that you free your
brother from the demands *you* placed on him.

You Are Changeless

You are the changeless Child of God; the extension of all God Is. To believe that you could be sick is to imagine that God could then be sick. The one who is sick is the character in the story you tell, the image of a self you have made that portrays you as a guilty person. Recognize this and what needs to be healed changes entirely. Now you realize it is only you who must decide if healing is justified.

To build defenses will not protect you from your enemies. But it will assure you of having enemies.

Welcoming a Forgiven World

If you want to give welcome to a loving brother and a loving world, then start today by laying its foundation in your determination to see the face of love that is everywhere around you now, but hiding behind a mask of guilt or fear. When this seems difficult, remember that what you see is not in the world, but in your mind, in the choice of what you want to find. Consciously want to see the Face of Christ. Now you can forgive what you thought you saw before and welcome a forgiven world into your loving presence.

A Perfect World

Our ego would like to experience a better world, if only "they" would change. The God Self suggests a perfect world already exists when I am ready to see past behavior (sin is not present in the Mind of God) and find the perfection in my brother.

When I try to solve a problem that seems to be "outside" of me, as in another person, it only reinforces the "bigger" problem of believing something *could be* outside of me.

Is It Possible Not To Love?

Thinking it is possible not to love is the basis for all our illusions of a false and distorted ego self. It is no more possible not to love than it is to be separate and it is only in our *story* of separateness that either does seem possible. In truth, love is the essence of who we are and the expression of our union. Because its purpose is Wholeness, it is indivisible and therefore has no opposite. In the ego's world, love is used to separate; to set those who deserve our love apart from those who don't. And because it expresses opposites, it even seems to co-exist with hate; moving us to sometimes love and sometimes hate the same person. Isn't it nice God gave us a substitute for our egos perception? Something we could trust to lead us to the Truth of what Love really is? We might even think about using it exclusively. Perhaps then we would remember, only in illusions is it possible not to love.

orgiveness Fast Track

When you discover a brother who appears to be unloving, whose behavior provokes fear or calls for a "slight" judgment, be grateful. Be grateful you have learned there is a different way to see him; that you have found the Means to see his loving presence just past his behavior. Be grateful you no longer need be burdened with the fears and anger of judging him – or yourself. Learning to make gratitude your first thought is the "fast track" to forgiveness.

Replacing The Ego's Perception

Forgiveness is not accomplished by expecting the ego's perception to overlook the guilt it sees in itself or anyone else. Forgiveness is asking for, and accepting, the evaluation of the God Self to replace the ego's perception entirely. Depending on perception is our attempt to bring truth to illusions, trying to make them real. But it is only through our appeal to the God Self that we will find what is real and true. Remember as you choose, illusions and fear go together, as do truth and love. Every choice for the God Self makes love more real than fear, for everyone.

Each time you are tempted to judge someone for anything, say, "I am sinless." Mean it and watch the need to judge "him" go away.

forgiving is the gift of love, for giving love unites the giver and who receives the gift as one.

The Real World

There is a "world" where nothing opposes love. It isn't now some far away place beyond our grasp. We can go there in an instant, the very moment we forgive someone we thought we could not love; the moment it dawns upon us we cannot change the Will of the One Who only loves and created us like Him. In this moment is our own desire to love released from sin's restrictions and freed to recognize Itself. In that moment is the world that love has made, but has been kept hidden by our "brother's" guilt, now free to be accepted and forgiven by everyone. Love now is recognized as all we want, for it alone expresses what we are.

The purpose of all relationships is to find the loving
Self we have disguised as a guilty brother.

The Light Of Love

There is no one in whom the Light of God's Love is not present. Whether of not I see it is the measure of how attached I am to the belief there is something wrong with me.

Message From Brother

"Let this time become a celebration of Who and What we are. Let us express our gratitude by sharing God's Gift to us with all those who are troubled and in pain. Let us hold the awareness of the Holy Spirits Presence in them that they may know their innocence and feel again God's Love for them as you extend them yours. Know as you give this gift it is the one thing that will heal all ills, bring peace to our troubled mind and restore the awareness of our one Self. Add your certainty to mine that it may become a light for all to see and follow. Then join with me in giving thanks to our Father for having given us this gift to give."

Discovering Your Self

Should you discover love in some new place, remind yourself it has always been there, just waiting to be found. Then recognize the same is true about discovering your Self.

Your Purpose

It is often good to re-examine our desire to have a helpful and loving purpose in the world. If it relies on the ego's need to correct an injustice or fix what is "wrong", we have again entrusted our healing to the source that sees a purpose for pain. It is easy to know when this happens for the ego's goals are conflicted, with no intention of ever being met. Our purpose here is to be witness to the truth of what is real and forgive the story we have made. For your "reality check," go to your place of refuge. Rest there with Him Who loves you. Assure Him of your willingness to love and your purpose has now been fulfilled.

As One Year Passes

As one year passes and another takes its place, I let my thoughts of sin and separateness, of fear and judgment, pass along with them. I choose now to accept instead my holiness, along with yours, and welcome a forgiven world into our mind. I choose to believe that uninterrupted peace and joy await us in this world and that every thought here begins with a love that draws us together. I trust that should I falter in my resolve, there is a light in us that you will hold for me until I have remembered. I know I do not make this choice alone, for that could never be. We go to truth together or we go there not at all. So take my hand as I take another. Together we form a network of love that will embrace and heal the world.

Awakening

The path to awakening seems long because we expect our ego's perception to correct itself. That is not going to happen but It can be immeasurably shortened if we forgive and let our God Self do the job God gave It to do.

Loving Is Natural

As long as you think it is possible to hate someone you are lost to the experience of being "naturally" loved. Seeking love from a source you perceive to be "outside" yourself is your admission it does not exist within you. And where love is not perceived there will be some form of hate, for it is through hate, or by its other name of fear, that the mind denies its natural desire is to love. It is as we remove each block to love and find love there to instantly take its place we come to learn the one thing that *is* "natural" about us. We are created in Love, by eternal Love and so eternal Love is what we are. This is the Will of God and so it has no opposite. Love is eternal. We are eternal because Love is what we are.

When Fear Arises

When fear arises it is because we have forgotten Who walks with us. Fear is the sense of being alone, which, in turn, only seems possible when we feel unloved or unloving. Learning to ask for guidance throughout the day, for even the most mundane choices, keeps us aware of the constant Presence of our holy and wholly loving Self. When the dark moments then seem to come we have the means to quickly move past them because we have established the reality of the Presence Whose only function is to help us and assure us that we are wholly loved and never alone.

"Understanding" Oneness

When we first begin to consider the reality of our oneness there are different intellectual concepts we investigate to understand what we instinctively believe to be true. But after a time it becomes apparent *there is no way* for the ego's perception to grasp the meaning or significance of what oneness represents. But when we turn our seeking over to our God Self, our need to understand gives way to a deeper, more "primal" desire – our fundamental need to love - everyone. Without this inclusive kind of Loving, oneness has no meaning. But with it the desire to join is perfectly natural. We were created by One Love to express this same One Love. In the Vision of our God Self there is nothing more to understand.

Healing Is Here Now

Healing is the recognition of what is now true. That means we already know it, even if it is hidden behind our misperceptions and the judgments we make. This is why it is so important to open our mind to what lies hidden there. The key to an open mind is the feeling of innocence. Guilt requires judgments, limiting our awareness to the scope of what we judge. Feeling there is something wrong with us creates fear, which narrows our thinking to our perception of what will keep us safe. Forgiveness reaches our sinlessness and opens our Mind to the awareness now hidden in our perception that Love can be divided and lost. Oneness is an abstract concept to a perception based on sin and separation. It is an easily accepted reality to one who looks for ways to take part in the adventure of Loving.

Judgment

When I judge anyone for anything at all it is my assertion that what *they* do controls my experience and thus empowers them to withhold the Peace of God from me. It may appear I have been first attacked without reason; that my judgment is in reaction to that attack. But it is only my thoughts that make my world what it seems to be. Had I not first judged myself sinful there would have been no thoughts of sin to project on my "attackers" and then return to me as an attack. I see the world through the lens of my self-perception the nature of which is to react to my beliefs, my judgment that sin is real. But I have another Source from which to make my choices, one that knows our sinlessness. I can choose to see us both in the Love God has for us; the Love that replaces our perception when I have no desire to judge. I can reclaim the Peace of God simply by accepting what is true.

Defenses Do Not Defend

Defenses are a double-edged sword. They do not keep us safe from danger for they must always fulfill their purpose of proving there is something we must defend against. Defenses look for reasons not to love. And always finds them. Forgiveness, on the other hand, opens the door to love and is never disappointed. Now is a good time to consider being defenseless.

Where Is Love?

To learn where love is, forgive the thought of sin.
Only the belief in sin and separation hides the
awareness that Love is everywhere.

The Truth of Co-Dependency

We are inter-connected expressions of an ever-expanding thought, completely dependent on each other to know the nature of our Self. Learning to recognize that we are whole is not about being complete as a separate individual. It is seeing ourselves as an integral part of all Creation. No one who sees himself as a separate and different individual can feel complete because he is dependent on his ties with the rest of Creation to truly know himself. Nothing that is a part of Creation can—in reality—even exist independent of the rest. Wholeness has no meaning if any part of it is missing. And the fundamental nature of Creation, being the Thought of God, is whole and complete.

Within the belief that we are separate, autonomous beings, everyone must feel there is something missing because the knowledge of what we are, is inherent in our Being. However, the need to project our guilt and be separate blocks our awareness that what is missing is the feeling of being connected to the very thing we are trying to be separate from.

Fairy Tales

Sin and guilt is an idea that should be treated lightly, like other fables and fairy tales. That is not easy to do when you feel the pain and suffering that comes from the physical experience of our belief that they are real. But the greatest legacy that sin's misperception leaves, is that it robs us of the memory of what love is.

The purpose of all relationships is to find the loving Self we have disguised as a guilty brother.

f

When ACIM tells us, *"Be vigilant only for God and His Kingdom,"* perhaps it means that when a loving thought comes into our mind, we should open our mouth and let it out. But when an unloving thought arrives we tap the "delete" key.

Saving The World

Saving the world does not need to be a long-term project. It will happen the moment we forgive our self-judgment and let our world become the mirror of what God created us to be. When we have withdrawn our judgments and let the Light of God's Love be reflected here, Heaven and earth will merge as one. Both the world and Heaven are a state of mind and you will "be" wherever you feel most at Home. Don't worry about needing to wait for "others" to also choose to awaken before you are free. It is the function of time to accommodate the purpose of our dreaming and it is only present in our dreams. Upon awakening we will find that nothing has changed since we seemed to fall asleep. All those we were afraid to leave behind are also as they were. It truly was just a dream.

The Light Of Love

There is no one in whom the Light of
God's Love is not present. Whether
or not I see it is the measure of how
attached I am to the belief there
is something wrong with me.

Where Do You Feel At Home?

We actually struggle to hold on to and keep ourselves in the hell of pain and sorrow. It is the world of death and destruction that we now claim as our "home." At the same time, we mightily resist accepting the peace and joy and love of Heaven that forgiveness offers us. We can choose which experience we want because we make the world we see.

We create a character that fulfills our ego's vision of who we think we are and then make a world where that character can feel at home. We choose this world of bodies and differences, conflicts and pain, where death seems an alternative to life and blocks the thought of Heaven. We look into the world we have made to replace Heaven and be the home of hate and think it is real and where we deserve to be. But Love has not abandoned us while we have turned away. Heaven has not ceased to exist in our denial of It. It is our world that is the dream. It is we who are asleep, not God. Change the world where you feel at home. Awaken to your holy presence by daring to love yourself. You cannot see anyone in Heaven until you do.

Heaven

Heaven, like this world, is a state of mind. This world reflects the belief that sin is real. What we refer to as Heaven is our memory of God and Creation as He created It. It is to see oneness in the many faces of Love. You cannot remember God until this is what you want to see everywhere. You must see God to recognize His Creation. Heaven is the "NOW" place in your mind, before the thought of sin and separation distorted the joy and love, the peace that shapes our natural awareness. It is time now. Come Home to Heaven. Forgive the world you see. Welcome the presence of every brother who sees himself sick and suffering and despised of God. Embrace him in the love you reserve for God that you may recognize the truth of both of us.

The prayer of forgiveness is a request that we be able to recognize what we already have.

Healing Is Not About Fixing What Is Broken

Healing is not learning how to fix something that is broken. It is recognizing that what God created whole and perfect is still whole and perfect now, unchanged by a dream that there is something wrong with us. When we attempt to heal a sickness in the body or correct a misperception we see in our brother's mind, we support the reality of that dream. Instead of looking for the thought that "caused" the sickness, or fixing our brother by correcting the misperception arising from his dream, ask the God Self to show you the beauty and perfection of God's Creation. Support the truth in both of you. Awaken the memory of God's changeless Love and bring to our consciousness the awareness that heals everything.

The difference between a saint and a sinner is in
our willingness to see clearly.

Perfect Happiness

God's Will for us is perfect happiness. It is for peace beyond anything the ego's perception can imagine. He has placed the Voice for Truth within our mind for us to hear and use to guide us in the choices that we make. But it is we who must make the choices in order to allow their benefits to be brought to us. Choose peace in the presence of fear and peace becomes our reality. Choose to love when love seems to have lost its way and we have become the Presence of love. Let the Voice for God choose through you and we have ended the separation we have imagined to exist in the world.

Become Defenseless

We are Beings of Spirit, Thoughts in the Mind of our Creator. Without the thought of sin, our brother is like us in every way. We live and function within the same Mind. We cannot change that so even our ego consciousness can only be separated by its misperceptions. We have the power to bring peace to every mind because all minds intermingle with our own and everyone wants peace exactly as we do, regardless of their behavior. Prove to yourself this is true. Become defenseless to one who seems to attack you and watch his attack melt away.

*f*orgiveness is the gift of love, for giving love
unites the giver and who receives the gift as one.

We are beginning now to realize we do not discover
who we are in contrast with one another, but by
recognizing how we are the same.

Wholeness

What makes you whole is the awareness that nothing exists
that is not present in you. This is the basis for what we call
"knowing." It is what gives meaning to what "Oneness" is.
This is the "Light" in us that makes darkness (imperfection
or lack) of any nature impossible. This is the condition of the
inner God Self.

forgive and find the joy in joyning.

f

Many Faces

There are many faces our ego consciousness brings to the world. There is the Nelson Mandela face, the Bashair al Assad face, the Mother Teresa face or the one we have called Genghis Kahn. Then there are the Larry, Suzie, John and Mary faces. And hidden beneath our need to be separate and different is another Face. It is the one that is unaffected by the appearances of bodies and the stories of sin they tell. It knows all these faces are the same. It knows that none of the stories are about "real" people. It holds clear the awareness that all God's creations are the same and filled with His grace. This One shares His Name with all the others and loves them all as One. This One we call the Face of God. Were we to see correctly we could also call It Mandela, Teresa, Larry or Suzie. Or . . .

Time – The Great Deceiver

Time is the great deceiver as we weave our dreams along what seems to be an evolutionary path. But dreams exist only to accommodate our beliefs and time is needed to distance us from past and future and hide the nature of our present and eternal Self.

The role time plays in our awakening to the truth of who we are is to separate the moment of falling asleep from the one where we awaken. This ensures there will be different paths to follow, progressive learning to unfold with many opportunities along the way for the ego's perception to remain in control and find ever more ways to make the dream seem real.

Outside our story there is no time. There is no "moment" between sleeping and waking, no distance to the path that would seem to lead us from one to the other. Yet because our belief in separateness is so great, we have pursued our awakening slowly, in stages we could more easily accept. But the momentum of our change is growing; we can now accept what only a short time ago was unacceptable. And one of the things that will quicken our pace still further is to bring to our consciousness the awareness that the dream we seem to struggle to overcome, has already ended. We follow a path that time has made, but backward from the point of its completion.

Journey Without Distance

Take a moment and envision what it would mean to already have reached your goal. Feel the release that comes from knowing there is no need to struggle. How much easier it will be not to judge or wonder if you will ever discover what it is like to be wholly loved.

We have always been able to make the choices that will free us from our judgments and our struggles, but just thinking there was somehow a need to first "make right" our sins or our mistakes, we justified the value of the path to get it done. But with that belief, there will always be a path, a reason not to be free.

Consider this idea. Give it some space to grow, to free you from the burden of wondering how to let go of your beliefs. Give it a chance to become part of your forgiveness attitude.

Save Your Brother From His Illusions

Save your brother from his illusions by loving him for who he is, not judging him for who he pretends to be. Save yourself from your illusions by loving your brother for who he is, not judging him for who you pretend he is. Save him to find yourself, for he can only be what you are. Forgive him today. He will not be more worthy tomorrow. Only our stories have changed. He is today as you have always been.

Love is present wherever love looks for it.

I Am As God Created Me

When the turmoil and suffering of the world appear overwhelming, this is the thought that restores our peace and sanity. What tries to join with fear and seems to suffer loss is not a part of who we really are. It is an image of a guilty, unloved self we have made that mocks the truth of who we really are. Today I will forgive this image I have made and free my mind to accept the truth. Today I will remember that I am free to love again!

Judging Behavior Is An Attack On Reality

Judging your brother for his behavior in a dream is an attack on the reality of your innocence. It also adds another layer of guilt to block the memory of our Oneness. We cannot find our own joyful and loving self while judging the brother who is a part of us. As long as we judge him guilty of anything, so must we suffer the effects of that judgment.

Who is brother or who is terrorist depends only on whether you decide they walk with you or they have a different purpose. Look for guilt and you open yourself to attack. Forgive and see a call for love and you will recognize what it is you want and offer them the same. We walk together and are free, or walk apart and lose ourselves in the gap that guilt has used to separate us.

I Am As God Created Me

There is a simple phrase whose truth will put an end to every dream of fear. We speak the words, "*I am as God created me,*" and , the possibility of pain, the thought of death, disappears into the awareness of what is true. Here, there is no story for guilt to tell, no thought to interrupt our perfect peace. "*I am as God created me.*" Now the darkness is dispelled from our one mind. There is lightness and a light in which we see the Presence of the Love of God. And know that all is well within the world as God created It.

When forgiving your worst enemy also forgive your best friend, to remind you the difference between them is only in your perception.

The Goal of forgiveness

It is good to be reminded the goal of forgiveness is to find there has never been anything to forgive. Our *"journey without distance,"* will end where it began, secure in the awareness we have never changed how God created us. This is difficult to see as the ego has focused only on validating its perception that there is something wrong with us. In the world of our perception, healing what is broken is a never-ending thing. Asking to be shown our perfectly created Self heals because it is the Vision of Christ. The Love of God abounds within us now, waiting only our forgiveness to be set free.

Two Ways To See

There are two entirely different ways for us to think and see. Both are motivated by what we expect to find. One looks for what is wrong because it sees through a veil of guilt and finds a world made to meet its expectations. The other looks for a light it dimly remembers but cannot find with eyes that see the world guilt has made. But we persist, as we must do, for we cannot be satisfied with less than what is true. Love looks for goodness within itself and then embraces all it sees with that vision, thus making everything like itself and part of what it is. You are the bringer of Light. You are the holder of Truth, the presence of Love. And yours are the choices that release our consciousness from fear.

Peace cannot be permanent until it is shared by everyone.

God or Ego?

Which is more important to you, God or the ego? Before you answer count the choices you made for God today as compared to those that supported your ego.

When you find a brother who cannot forgive himself, do it for him. He is, after all, part of you.

Heaven is the experience that all wills are joined, that its soul purpose and its only function is to love.

Every judgment we forgive removes another
"reason" for us to be unhappy.

No Need To Die

The world is changing. It will soon reflect a different perception from what we now see. One of the most dramatic changes we will note is that there will be those who find no need for the body to die. Not because we have found some miraculous way to save it, or because it is important to who and what we are. This will happen because we are accepting it is irrelevant to who we are and we are finding less need to maintain our separateness from one another.

I say this in spite of what seems to be the escalation of hatred and violence we are seeing in the world. It is important to remember that what "happens" in the world is what we expect to find there. It is of our making and we will find what we are looking for. Do we need more of an incentive to look for love.

"Seeing is believing," is the egos motto, but it is just the opposite that is true.

Condemning God?

The next time you feel compelled to condemn someone for what has happened in the world, ask yourself if you would condemn God for what your brother seems to have done. The world is a story we tell, a dream we have of happenings that have no meaning and no effect on anything outside that story. As surely as God is not a part of our story, neither is the brother we have judged. What we judge is only a broken and distorted caricature of him and of our Self. The one we think we judge is not there. But as long as we persist in judging him we will think that it is he and hold ourselves apart and miss the joy of loving him and feeling loved by God.

What Does Our Brother Want?

What does our brother or our sister really want of us? It's easy to be deceived. But no matter how it looks, you will find it is exactly what you want of them. We have tried to project our self-guilt onto them to make them worse or better than we. And they have done the same. But when we realize we both are looking to be loved we will find the love within ourselves to give and join with them.

Changing The Body's Purpose

To heal the body we must change its purpose. We use it now to illustrate our separateness and punish our guilt, insuring it must ultimately be sick and die. We judge our brother for our sins that we now see in him and welcome his attack as means to share our guilt. With forgiveness we can show our brother we see no sin in him. Without the goal of guilt there is nothing to be punished. Without the thought of sin there is nothing to hide the Presence of God's Love and healing takes the place of death. The body's purpose now becomes a witness to the life we share together.

To Love And Be Loved

To forgive, it is fundamental to know there is no one who does not have the desire to love and to be loved. This comes from a knowing in the deepest part of our Being that Loving is natural and necessary to be happy and free to live beyond the limits of fear. The desire to Love is the foundation of our Being and it will blossom into our awareness as we release the judgments we now use to separate us from it.

When forgiving your worst enemy also forgive your best friend, to remind you the differences between them are only in your perception.

A world of conflict arises from every choice that supports guilt. Heaven awaits those who know this is a choice you cannot make.

The perfect response to an urge to judge is laughter.

Learning

All of our learning is ultimately dependent upon accessing our inner awareness of the truth and relying on it to develop new habits of thinking. This (God Self) awareness is in our mind now, but being unfamiliar to our perception it can seem unreachable. But if we are persistent our desire to know cannot be denied. Unlikely as it may now appear, in truth, we are at the center of all knowing, at all times. It is only our perception that minds are individual and independent that hides this truth from us. Without this confusion all thought is known to be interconnected and flowing to a common, loving purpose.

Lack

If there consistently seems to be something lacking in your world it must be because you believe there is something lacking in you. We see the world as a mirror for how we see ourselves. If you would be free of lack in your world you must learn there is nothing missing in you. Any lack must ultimately be recognized as a belief there is a lack of love. Everything we attempt to get from the world is substitute for the love we feel is missing within us. To learn there is no love missing in you, turn to those in your life you have judged to be lacking in some way. Ask your God Self how to show them there is no lack of love in them. Giving to others what you think is missing in you is the best way to discover what you really have.

Self Acceptance

Every reason not to love others disappears with self-forgiveness. The urge to judge anything is gone when you have accepted yourself. All the symbols of separateness depend upon a single thought: There must be something wrong with me. Forgive this thought. Ask to see the whole and complete "you" the God Self sees, not the one that "needs" to be healed. Now is the Vision of a forgiven world free to rise. Now we are free to love everyone.

To Have Peace Give Peace

If we want to have a world where peace and happiness are all that we expect, then we must be willing to offer only peace and happiness to everyone. The world will always be a mirror of what we see within. And if we want this peace and happiness now, then now is when we must be willing to give it. Nothing will happen tomorrow that would make us want it more, or make anyone more deserving to have it.

We Walk Together

No matter how it appears, we walk together in this world where we all seem separate. We call no one "enemy" or "friend" who is not, in truth, a part of who we are. No one suffers or is completely free apart from all the rest. We can be sure that we share with everyone our desire to find the path to love, simply because we are all a part of the same consciousness, and all created from the same Love.

Perception

All perception is an accommodation to accept as "true" whatever validates our core belief. And our choice to want it to be true is all that is required to make our misperceptions appear to be fact. That is the power of our mind. It is the only real power in all Creation, whether used for illusions or for truth.

Our Relationship With God

All relationships have the potential to reflect our relationship with God. The Light of God's Love is "born" in everyone at the instant of their creation. As deeply as it may be hidden under the layers of our Self-denial, it is immediately available to us in the Vision our God Self holds. It is this Light, this Love, that is the basis for all our seeking, and it is revealed to us as we forgive the stories in which It has been lost. Ask simply to see the spark of God's Love that has blossomed into your brother and you will recognize what makes you One with hi

I have never really judged the world but only accused it of what I feel guilty about.

Condemning

If you believe you can condemn someone you have also subjected yourself to being condemned and you will suffer whatever effects your belief deems appropriate for him or her to suffer. Such is the law of perception. Forgiveness will withdraw the judgment and free both of you from the consequences you would have imposed.

The cost of really changing your mind is the admission that nothing you now believe is true.

Giving and Receiving

Judgment proclaims that guilt is valued more as a tool for healing than is love. Forgiveness is a gift acknowledging there is no guilt. You choose which will rule your life by what you offer others.

Projection and Responsibility

Nothing will really change until we take responsibility for what we have projected onto others. It is my thoughts that make my world, whether I claim them for myself, or judge them in others. But until I acknowledge they are "mine" I will have no control over them and feel no power to change them.

Forgive and find the joy in joyning!

Truth and Happiness

Happiness isn't found by looking for the perfect relationship or for the perfect job. Having everything the world offers will not make you happy. Happiness is all about being satisfied with yourself. So forgive yourself, find your truth and discover how much there is for you to be happy about!

Undefended Loving

Undefended loving opens the mind to opportunities for a broader range of happy relationships, beyond those sought to satisfy ego desires and needs. Judgment limits mind's function to the ego's goals of separation. It severely restricts our mental health and also limits the body's ability to function without pain. The alternative: forgive and be happy!

The Reward Of Forgiveness

When any two consciously choose to engage with the God Self together, the effects far exceed what could occur if each had done so alone. Feeling the wholeness, the completeness of all things comes with the simple intention to join with what is part of you, however long denied. And joining in the Presence of the God Self also brings the Vision, the awareness of Love's Presence, to you. In that instant when you are free of the idea of sin and the need to be different you see the magnitude of what the oneness of Love really is. In but a moment you are aware there has been nothing but an untrue thought of sin that seemed to separate you from Paradise Itself. This is the "reward" of forgiveness, finding what was hidden but never lost.

Love Surrounds Us

All around us there is only love, when we have eyes to see it. Don't be discouraged if you cannot see or feel it yet. Our ego need to keep its guilt still seems strong, seeming even to strengthen as we feel closer to our goal. Our inclination is to intensify our efforts to move past these feelings, to resist our resistance to surrender. And because our resistance only strengthens what we resist, disappointment sets in. Focus instead on the one thing we do not resist: The desire to be loved. This desire will find the Place in us until it is fulfilled, for we have asked to recognize our will and God's are one. Now can we move past the belief our guilt is real.

Together we form a network of love that will embrace and heal the whole world.

Unreasonable Loving

Despite all appearances, loving without reason is the most natural thing we do. Peace is our "normal" state of mind. Happiness is the "default" condition when guilt has been let go. This is the changeless reality that exists just below our "un-natural" thoughts of sin and separation. When we choose to look for what is "right" not "wrong," we discover there was peace and happiness there all along.

The Choice For Love

The ego would have us use our brother by sharing our guilt with him. God sees him as co-creators with us, to extend His Love and so ensure completion of Himself. What stands between the ego's goal and the Will of God is a thought called "sin." An untrue thought, but strong enough to make a world of pain and sorrow, providing that is what we want. But, the only strength the ego really has is what we give it; its only power a measure of what we really want or think that we deserve. Ask to be shown how to have what you really want. Let forgiveness become your goal and see how this makes Love a choice more easily made than fear.

Where Are You?

Understanding all the implications of what is meant by Jesus telling us that this world is a "dream," a story we are telling about who we think we are, is most times hard to fathom. He tells us that the world is not "real," that it exists only in our imagination. If this is true, if we are not "in" our story, if we are not "in" the body playing its role in the story, where are we? Can we even find the answer to this question in the awareness of the character in the story?

For most who are seeking the truth, we believe the answer will be found in remembering we are a different "Self." I suggest that "who" we are is made vastly more difficult to remember because we continue to insist that "where" we are in a "place" that makes it impossible to know the answer. Cont'd

Where Are You? (Cont'd)

We are told that we are beings of spirit, not confined to the limitations of the body or the world. How are we to learn that this is true if we continue to make choices as though we "live" inside the confines of our story? If we are ever to create an experience that our story is untrue we must begin to recognize that we are not "in" that story.

If we cannot know "where' or "who" we are from within our current perception, how will we ever find it? This is why God placed the awareness of the Holy Spirit, the God created Self, in our Mind, so that we would always know exactly where, and who, we are. Using the guidance of this Presence is how we come to know our Self.

Nurturing the Presence of this God Self is what builds trust and confidence there, instead of with the ego's perception by continuing to use it to make our choices. This means choosing to use the GS for *all* our choices, It is not there for us to use just when we are in "trouble or to relieve our pain. It is to learn through practice that there is an entirely different way to think; a different world to experience. Continuing to rely on the ego's judgment for "non spiritual" matters only strengthens our belief that there is some value in maintaining our separateness.

Using the God Self Awareness is what will allow a loving world to replace the one we now "see." Using the God Self Awareness will connect us to the whole Self and there will be no question "where" we have always been.

The Gift of Joining

You could not give a greater gift to anyone than to recognize your mind is one with theirs. We do not yet realize the joy we would feel in accepting our brother as our self until we recognize his mind as part of ours. We have no sense of what it is to be free until we have experienced this joining. We cannot know the Love of God until we have accepted it for everyone.

Have you ever felt unconditionally loved? Are you willing to love completely and without condition? Each of these feelings depends upon the other.

Self-Acceptance

Every reason not to love others disappears with self-forgiveness. The urge to judge anything is gone when you have accepted yourself. All the symbols of separateness depend upon a single thought: There must be something wrong with me. Forgive this thought. Ask to see the whole and complete "you" the God Self sees, not the one that "needs" to be healed. Now is the Vision of a forgiven world free to rise. Now we are free to love everyone.

The Hoax

We have a choice for the kind of world we live in. Since time began, we have been perpetuating a hoax upon ourselves, living a life of uncertainty, at times of indescribable pain, of suffering, fear and an endless search for peace and love. In truth, everything we need to live in peace and happiness is within us right now. Have you ever wondered why we keep looking?

Bring The Ego's Intention To The God Self

When I perceive myself as separate and "individual" and attempt to change "my" mind, only my story of being separate and different is affected. When I recognize that my story is only a different version of all stories, then ask our God Self to use my intention to change our consciousness, that change will affect all of consciousness because His Vision of me is as a part of the whole. Using my ego's perception to change the way I see does nothing to free others from the idea that separation is real. But all change implemented by the God Self affects the whole consciousness because He sees it all as one. Our function is to bring the egos intention to Him, desiring the change, but trusting Him to make it for the benefit of all.

Correcting Perception

To the ego, the learning process is one of correcting our perception, not letting it go. This is our attempt to make something real / true out of what is not real or true - simply because *that is what we want it to be.* Real change can only occur when we surrender our perception entirely. Resisting the temptation to believe that our perception can "grow" into truth is paramount to achieving true knowledge. It would not have been necessary for us to be given the Presence of the God Self were it possible for our perception to evolve into the truth. The body is itself, a characterization of our perception. Its purpose is to make separation real. As long as we think it is part of us, its existence will limit the reality of our ability to join. To let our perception go also means we must be willing to let the thought that is our body go with it, for the two are the same.

What Makes A Problem A Problem?

Here is an exercise that can be very enlightening, is fun to do and can, coincidently, change your life.

Each day for a week count all the opportunities you can find to forgive and bring a loving intention to answer what you had perceived as a problem. Be creative. Try each day to best the day before. Do this with friends. Help one another when something seems unforgivable. At weeks end take a moment to contemplate if you are happier than the week before.

At the end of the week it will likely have begun to become evident there actually is no problem for which love is not the only answer on which we can rely. This, in turn, leads to an amazing revelation: What makes a problem a problem is only when we are not willing to see love as the answer.

Forgive the world and you have changed its purpose from judgment to joy. Forgive yourself and you have found the freedom to love unconditionally.

Defenses

Defenses strengthen what they defend against. They cannot make you safe for your need for them assures that you will be attacked. Understanding that we make the world by projecting our guilty thoughts outward, we can see how all defenses are actually invitations to be attacked.

Free Will

Free will within the ego's perception is drastically over-rated. Since the ego will not choose for love it is limited only to those choices its perception will accommodate, namely those that promote sin and separation. You might begin to wonder if it has any value at all. In fact, when I think of the choices I have made that have brought me peace, and all those that have brought something else, I think I will confine my free will to choosing to accept God's Will for me. Even if it means I will be peaceful and loving all the time.

What Is Healing?

When I am sick or experiencing any of fears effects, the experience seems real and so the thought of healing comes from the belief that something is broken and needs to be fixed. Here I must remember that it is necessary for the God Self to be the One in charge of healing because He is not confused by the seeming reality of sickness or fear. He does not try to fix what is not broken and would only make the illusion real, changing nothing. He corrects the illusion by seeing that nothing real happened; our real Self was never threatened. Changing our perception will change the form of our illusion, but it is the God Self Vision of the truth of our perfect wholeness that dissolves that perception entirely and heals what we see and experience. Our healing mantra then becomes, "Please show me the loving self, the perfect wholeness I already have.

We spend much of our time, in sometimes painful ways,
trying to make ourselves lovable. There is another way.
Simply say to your God Self, "I am willing to be loved."
Mean it, and love will come to you.

Gifts of God

We cannot lose the Gifts of God, no matter how we seem to try. It is only our denial that we deserve them that seems to prevent our having them. To find what is hidden beneath your denial, to make plain the Gift that is yours, open your heart to everyone, all the time. Be willing to give what you look for to know where it really is. Only in this way is your denial denied.

Power of the Mind

We have no real concept of the power of our mind to create or to heal because we have abdicated our power to the belief there is something wrong with us. Freeing us to use it again requires that we begin to forgive the idea that our guilt is real; to assume that we have not changed what God created us to be. For one hour take the image of everyone who crosses your mind to the Presence of your God Self and ask to see only what is true about them. What you see thereafter in the world will never be the same.

A World That Love Has Made

Wanting only a world that love has made is important to the journey taken here. It reminds us that "letting love in" is a choice we always have. And when we understand it is our brother's deepest wish as well, what had seemed before to be our resistance to his beliefs is no longer an obstacle to our loving and joining with him.

You Cannot Decide "Who" You Will Love

When you think of yourself as separate, believing that your concerns and desires are different from others, you cannot interact—cannot join— with anyone, even those you might think you want to be close to. The ego does seem to be able to decide on who it will accept and those it must reject because the differences are too great. But in truth the need to be separate does not permit selectively choosing who is worth loving and who must fall short of your approval. That is decided when you accept or reject yourself.

The need to be separate begins with the rejection of yourself and the belief that there is something wrong with you. This then becomes the way you see the world, for you see everything through the same perception that you see yourself. In this one thing is the ego perfectly consistent.

Become aware that every judgment made condemns, not just yourself, but every thing else God has Created as well. And remember too each time you refuse to accept your story of guilt and fear as being true, your forgiveness frees you to see another world. And here, without the judgment of yourself, you are free to join, free to know the joy that comes with remembering what it is like to love indiscriminately!

Think for a moment what it would be like to go about your day with your mind filled only with happy and loving thoughts. Everyone you meet has a smile and a glow of happiness about them. There is no sickness, no hunger, no conflict or lack; no striving, no blame, no expectations, no time and no death. Peace has replaced fear everywhere in this world. There is no word to describe hate for all the reasons not to love are gone. This is our mind without the thought of sin. This is our world when we see no guilt to judge.

Perfect Happiness

Our thoughts have long enough supported a world of suffering and hate. We have been ignorant of what is really true and of our ability to change what is not true. God's Will for us is perfect happiness, not sacrifice or penance. We can end the ego's journey and accept the means God has given us to share His peace and joy - right now. Go to The God Self and ask that it be so.

Love's Purpose

Love loses its meaning, its very purpose, in separateness. Love is Creation extending Itself with the unshakable assurance it will forever be the same. Here is our truth that peace and joy are never lost; that Heaven is a forever Place. We do not lose Loves Presence in our Mind in our stories of being separate, but we do deprive ourselves of the incredible peace and joy our acceptance of it brings. Consider for a moment that there is no one you would not love in the innocence of their creation. Now forgive your story of separateness and time and let that moment live again.

Two Ways To See

There are two entirely different ways for us to think and see. Both are motivated by what we expect to find. One looks for what is wrong because it sees through a veil of guilt and finds a world made to meet its expectations. The other looks for a light it dimly remembers but cannot find with eyes that see the world guilt has made. But it persists, as it must do, for it cannot be satisfied with less than what is true.
Then in a quiet moment it hears a voice that whispers: *Look within to find your innocence and the love you seek. Then embrace all you see within that vision, allowing everything to be like yourself and part of what you are. You are the bringer of the Light. You are the experience of God Loving. Give freely to everyone all that you ask for from God. Yours are the choices that release our consciousness from fear.*

Where will you find a sinless world? The same place you found the one dedicated to hate and blame and guilt—in your perception. Which you accept as real depends on what you think is true about yourself. Forgive yourself and set the world free.

Free To Love

You are free when you are without the need to judge; when there is no reason not to love. Being without the need to judge comes with the recognition there is nothing wrong with you, no reason for you not to be loved. It is here we finally begin to realize what love really is.

Heaven is the awareness that all minds are joined and that their purpose and soul function is to love.

Grace of God

The Grace of God has already been given us. We have it now, and cannot lose it but our sense of guilt blocks our awareness and acceptance of It. Forgive the thought that there is any story your brother could tell that would make him unworthy of your love, and you have freed him by God's Grace and joined him there. Expose yourself to what you have by giving it away.

Our Chaotic Mind

We are not at home among our thoughts that look for fault, that anticipate pain and put us in isolation from one another. In this world we wander among an ever-shifting stream of fearful, contradicting thoughts that lead nowhere. We wonder why peace seems so elusive, joy so quickly lost. The simple truth is our mind is filled with chaos because of the conflicted judgments we constantly make; judging everything we see because we have condemned the one who sees it.

Lack

Every form of lack, be it lack of money, lack of self-worth or lack of peace, arises from the belief that there is something lacking in us. We think we are unlovable. When we know that we are loved it is impossible to think anything is missing. To know that you are loved forgive every reason you can find not to love someone else. Be grateful for each discovery, for every release brings you closer to the freedom of feeling wholly fulfilled.

We are the creators of our universe. Whether we have created it from loving or fearful thoughts will determine if it is a loving or a fearful place.

Loving and Being Loved

Is there something about the world that could justify my not loving it? Is there something about the world that I have not made? When I can finally answer "no" to both of these I will know why I can only feel loved to the extent that I am willing to love.

Real forgiveness

The miracle of real forgiveness is discovering the freedom that comes with accepting that part of your Self you had previously condemned. It is learning that releasing a brother from "his" guilt is the same as releasing you from yours. We are part of a single consciousness, as inter-connected in our common story about sin and separation as we are in God's Creation. Believing we can awaken alone is like imagining one thought in our mind could change while another which confirmed it remained as before.

To free ourselves from fear we must remember that fear is only possible when love seems missing. Yet where is there for love to go when it is the foundation of who we are? When fear arises then, no matter what seems to be its cause, know it is your call for love. Then ask for the opportunity to love another as you wish to be loved.

From Brother:

I recently ask our Brother about something he purportedly said. I thought you might enjoy his response:

"The saying, 'No man comes to the Father except through me,' was misunderstood. What I was attempting to convey was the futility of trying to find God "alone." It is only your sense of needing to be alone that serves to keep you in a place seemingly apart from Him. My encouragement was to invite everyone to join with me that in our union we would find Him together. When you join with a brother you let go the need to be separate and in your joining recognize the Presence of the One Who created you both as a part Him."

Love Is Everywhere

Love is everywhere I choose to see it for Love created everything that lives and created it like Itself. When I do not see love it is because I have chosen to ignore what Love created and tried to make of it something of my egos choosing. When hate or suffering is what I see I have tried to replace Loves Presence with my story of sin. It is important that I remember love does not come and go. Love is everywhere I bring it, for love is what I am.

The mind is not contained within the body. Just the opposite is true.

Self orgiveness

We long to be free of the fearful thoughts that plaque us. We look for distraction in the things we do. We may even try surrendering our thoughts to our God Self. But until we have forgiven the only one we ever have really judged our perception of guilt will persist, and our thoughts will all justify that which we fear is true.

The Power Of Intention

There is within us the perfect Guide to peace and happiness.
We mostly, however, misunderstand Its purpose. We think
our peace and happiness depend on the *things* we choose
and so we look for guidance for what we do. And so we are
frequently frustrated when we cannot hear which choice to
make. We have forgotten all things will serve the purpose we
have given them. They will ultimately fulfill or disappoint us
based solely on the goal that we have given them. Recall how
frequently Jesus advises us that to see something differently
we must change the purpose we have given it.

When you seek guidance, then, about which choice to make,
ask what hidden purpose you have already given to the
choice rather than what you think you want from the choice,
for that is what will determine its outcome for you. When you
decide what outcome you want, the choice you make must
bring it to you. Ask to be given the willingness to receive
peace and happiness. Ask to be shown how to offer peace
and happiness to others. Both of these will then bring peace
and happiness to you.

A *f*orgiven World

Do take your belief to your God Self. But do so with the intention of surrendering not your thoughts, but the belief itself that there is something wrong with you. Forgive yourself and your thoughts will then support a forgiven World.

You will feel totally loved when it is your desire to totally love.

f

A Willingness to Love

Who must set the time for awakening but we who pretend to be asleep? We do not know the steps to reach our goal, for that we must be led. But it is we who must recognize when we are drawn to pursue the ego's goals, like when my awakening seems disconnected from yours. I must remember then that the paths we walk are all the same, guided by a single Source to the same outcome. It is here I will see I can only accept being loved to the extent that I am willing to love.

There Is No Sin

There is no sin. When I identify what I see as sin it is an attack upon the truth of who I am. It means I have closed my mind to love and denied I can awaken to the truth. But when I forgive I firmly state that it is not God's Will that we be damned and I would join with Him in offering freedom to the world that sin has made. When I forgive I affirm that I am free to love unconditionally and available to awaken to the truth. There is a simple way to recognize the Will of God: It always insists upon loving. Whatever else it must convey is then received with love. This must be true for us to recognize it is God's Love that connects us and only by our loving will we recognize being connected to the Self we seek. Therefore, when we are in doubt about what to do or say, we need only remember to set our intention to be loving to know that our will and the Will of God is one.

Truth of Oneness

forgiving what we have judged and refusing to judge it again, changes our belief that guilt is justified because it brings us peace and makes us happy. Feeling unconditionally loved opens our heart to loving unconditionally and dispels the idea that sacrifice and suffering play any part in awakening to the truth of our Oneness.

Healing Sickness

Healing is not about seeing someone fixed that I perceive to be sick. Healing is holding the Holy Spirit's Vision that, in truth, they remain as perfect as God created them. Healing is not about fixing our story. It is about remembering the truth and letting the story go.

forgiveness does require practice before we will place as much trust there as we have given to our judgments. But as we do and as it grows, our willingness to find the truth will grow with it.

I am as God created me.

I am as God created me. When the turmoil, uncertainty and suffering of the world appear overwhelming, this is the thought that restores our peace and sanity. What tries to join with fear and seems to suffer loss is not a part of me. It is an image of a guilty, unloved self I have made that mocks the truth of who I really am. Today I will forgive this image and free my mind to accept the truth. Today I will remember that I am free to love again!

The Two-Way Mirror

The ego's world is like a two-way mirror. It reflects from the inside - out all of its beliefs of what it perceives is wrong. It then sees these beliefs from the other side, the outside, as though its "sins" belonged to the world and it now must suffer their effects. Seeing like this, it then believes it is the victim of the world that it has made. It still suffers the payment guilt demands but at the hand of an avenging world and not its own. Is this insane, or what?

Becoming Defenseless

There is no one who does not want to be happy and at peace, no one who does not want to be loved. Yet, the world we now see seems to be becoming progressively more chaotic. This is not because we are "regressing"; they are the thought forms that are expressing our fear of becoming defenseless, as we move closer to our willingness to join. Be encouraged that any time one of us chooses to be loving where we have previously condemned, peace and happiness is more easily chosen by everyone.

One Consciousness

If there is someone you perceive that does not see the truth of who they are, how often have you wondered what you can do to help? In truth, we need only find and accept the truth of who we are for ourselves. In that awareness is all consciousness transformed to what it was before the world of separation began. And in that moment, out of time, the Vision of the one Self registers everywhere and for an instant our one consciousness knows Itself, without exception.

We Are Not Alone

We tirelessly search the world for what can make us happy, keep us safe and bring us love. We commit the self we see to making it our home. Yet there is nothing "here" to satisfy our real longing. We are not at home where separateness and differences seem to define us. But even in our world we are not alone. God's Hand extends to us from our brother, though it often seems intent on pushing us away. Take his hand with your desire to know that God walks with you and the purpose of the world has changed. What we have feared has become an invitation to love. God's Gift is recognized at last; our searching now is done.

You Are The One

It is not you who can be sad or sick. It is not you who resists being loved. That is only the character in the charade we play. You are the one who seems to sleep, but is untouched by dreams of any kind. You are the one who will remember and awaken and hold the truth for everyone. You are the one that is part of God and part of me.

The Present Moment

To stay in the present moment, accept yourself now. When you accept yourself as innocent and complete in this moment there is nothing in the past to judge and nothing for you to become in the future. Now you are free from the need for time.

Daily Prayer

Amidst all of our uncertainties and challenges our daily prayer need only be, *"Let me know all things exactly as they are."* We can free ourselves from the stress and fear of yet another variation of what will satisfy the ego's needs by remembering that finding peace and happiness, being free of lack and pain, does not come from our efforts for "self improvement." These are attacks on what God has created whole and perfect. All that we must change is the mistaken idea that there is something about us that we must change.

What Am I Witness To?

What I am witness to in the world defines who I think I am.
When I describe the world as being in turmoil and as a place
of suffering and feel the fear these thoughts engender, I am
a witness to a self-made of fear. And my world will continue
to bear the fruit of that perception. But when I remember I
did not create myself, that I have never had the opportunity
to do more than misperceive the truth, I can begin to see
instead a call for love and recognize the gift of love I have to
give.

The Purpose Of The World

We have made the world then given it the purpose to punish
and imprison us, to justify our fears and teach us the danger
of trusting love. In it we see our one consciousness divided
into bodies that cannot join, that suffer pain and die. Yet, it
is we who have made this world from our thoughts of guilt.
Its only purpose now is to serve that guilt. But we can forgive
the world by changing the goal we have given it. When love is
all we want for everyone it can become a "place" where love
and happiness abounds.

What Comes First

What comes first: The way someone treats me, or my expectation of it? We cannot be too often reminded that our primary challenge in changing our experience in the world is to change what we are looking for and what we expect to find. Is it possible to find only love in the world I now see? Can I trust what someone would do if I just loved them? If you feel it is worth the "risk" to find out, say to your God Self, *"I am willing today not to be afraid of love. Help me."* Then know that you have changed the course of your world.

When we forgive ourselves and our guilt is gone, we will see nothing in all world we do not love.

The Cause Of Sin

The cause of sin is kept alive by the belief in differences. The thought of sin would not long survive your acceptance of your brother being exactly like you. Without the ego's belief in sin there would be no need to be different from him, nothing to block your awareness of the bond of love that connects us all as one. Ask how to see that everyone's interest is your own; that the love they seek comes from the same Place you will find it. There is a place within your mind where differences do not exist. Go there when you feel ready to accept the Peace of God. Go there when you are ready to know that you are loved.

The Penalties of Guilt

Pain and suffering are the penalties of guilt. They are also the price of ignorance for guilt is optional, being self-imposed. Peace and joy and love are not the prize achieved for becoming a better person. They are the "option" when forgiveness replaces guilt as what we want. Only our thoughts can hurt us. Both attack and forgiveness may seem to focus on someone else, but their seeds are planted in our own mind, and it is there they both will first bear fruit.

forgiveness satisfies The Egos Needs

While it is judgment that seems best to serve the egos purpose, it is forgiveness that finally satisfies its need. Condemnation does confirm its sinful self-image, but it is the desire to know that we are loved that underlies its every goal. Rather than resist and condemn your ego, give it what it *really* wants.

The Choice For Love

The world is what I make of it. My experience is determined by what I want to find there. When love is all I want to find my ego's perception will no longer distort my intentions or falsely confuse me as to its source. In our sane mind, we are creators of Truth and extend Truth simply by "seeing" it. So I can safely say, the entire world depends on whether I choose to look for love - or something else.

Love Has No Measure

When you find yourself expressing to someone close to you, consciously expand your intention to include a few others you may not know so well. As they settle more firmly in your mind begin to add others you may not "know" at all. And finally include everyone in God's Creation. Sit with the feeling this brings you. You are teaching yourself that love has no limits, does not discriminate where to begin or end. Slowly you will notice a feeling of love enveloping you. Your Love has joined you with everyone it touched and you have discovered the power and truth of Oneness. Now bask in the knowing that every loving thought that has ever existed in the Mind of God – was meant for you.

Changing The World

There is nothing in the world that can make us happy or sad, peaceful or afraid. For we have given all things all the meaning that they have. "They," in fact could not exist without the purpose we have for them. And the purpose of the world we see is to support the image of the ego self that we have made. To change our world, then, we must let go our concept of the self that it supports. To find a world that we can love we first must learn to forgive and love the self that made it.

Am I Willing To Love?

There is a question we each must ultimately answer. Am I willing to love and be loved - completely? Will I surrender myself totally to peace and experience a Presence of eternal joy? These are not feelings to be idly wished for at some obscure and future time. This is how we would naturally feel the very moment our mind is free of guilt. And the miracle of real forgiveness is that this moment is waiting for us right now!

Unreasonably Happy

If you are looking for reasons to be happy in the ego's story of the world, you won't find them. In this world there are an infinite number of reasons to be angry, fearful or sad. None to be happy for no reason at all. Fortunately there is also nothing in the ego's story that is real or true. So if you want to be "unreasonably" happy, join with your God Self and step outside your dream. Here ego reasons cease to exist. They are replaced with the knowing that only love is real and you are the Presence of Perfect Love. Can you be happy with that?

The journey to Truth seems long because of the distance we keep between us.

The Power Of The Choice For Peace

From the perspective of separate minds, it is impossible to understand how your intention to let go your defenses and choose to join with someone can change their motivation to attack you. Seen through the awareness of a shared consciousness, it is apparent nothing else could occur. Let us remember we can influence the conflict in the world with every choice we make for peace.

*f*orgive the world you see. Learn to travel light. The time it takes to get to Heaven is directly influenced by the amount of baggage you carry.

You Cannot Decide What Is True

Even a Child of God cannot decide what is true because Who and What He is, is the truth and He did not create Himself. But having denied our identity there is one thing we must decide: Do we want to know the truth? Believing we are "sinful," we have made a perception to take the place of truth, thinking that the truth would condemn us. Now we must decide which is real and which we want. We literally make that choice with each decision whether to judge or to forgive. It cannot be too strongly stated, every judgment makes sin real and keeps us prisoner to its despair. And every forgiving thought turns an enemy into a friend and in the joining allows love to remember what is true.

The source of all our fears is our mistaken belief that there is something wrong with us. We have created a belief we are willing to die for and it isn't even true. What could be more insane?

The Whole and Holy Child of God

The miracle of real forgiveness is when we find the whole and holy child of God that we have hidden in the dream of pain and sorrow. We do not see it now for we see the world through the perception of what we believe is wrong with us. We do not yet believe there is another world waiting only on our desire to find it. We have not yet accepted that the world lives solely in our mind. We cannot yet grasp there is nothing that separates us from peace and love and joy except our belief we do not deserve to have them.

Connecting

Learning to connect with others and feel the sense of joy and safety that brings us is how we begin to overcome the ego's need to be autonomous. But we cannot connect to the "things" or forms of the world that are the symbols of our separateness. We cannot relate to being joined to a tree, an animal or even another human form. But we can relate to being part of a consciousness that is trying to justify its belief in separateness and differences by expressing as a tree, an animal or a different person. Recognizing it is the same consciousness will begin to bring a better awareness of what oneness means.

Learning and Listening

The difference between learning lessons and listening to guidance is often confusing. The idea of lessons comes from the ego's belief there is something broken that needs to be fixed. It most frequently leads to, and satisfies the ego's need to "do" something to solve its problems. Guidance through forgiveness teaches that healing occurs simply by seeing differently. Clearing the mind of judgments previously made frees it to find the Presence of your loving Self. It is the process of "undoing." Lessons begin with the feeling there is something wrong. Forgiveness teaches there is nothing to judge.

f

Joining

We cannot expect to know what joining is really like within the story of separateness. There is no joining when we feel a need to measure ourselves by such things as intelligence or skill, charisma or the desire to financially succeed, or any other standard whose purpose is to point out differences. The purpose of everything within the world that separation has made must make separation seem real. But it is the desire for "someone else" to share our guilt that gives separation its real power. As we learn to forgive and accept the unreality of sin and guilt there will be no reason not to love your brother, or yourself,

Motivation to forgive

I am motivated to forgive when I remember that when guilt is gone from my belief it has ceased to exist, for it has never been present in the Mind of God.

When forgiving what someone seems to have done is difficult, it is likely because you think <u>your</u> sins are unforgivable.

Authenticity

If you accept the world as authentic then what you do there defines your worth and who you are. If you judge what you have done as bad you will see yourself as a bad person with the need to atone for what has made you bad. Unfortunately, once you have judged yourself your guilt will remain, for in the ego's judgment there is no atonement. Forgiveness denies the reality of guilt and changes the world's purpose by allowing the natural desire to love to replace the need to judge and in the presence of love you will know what is authentic.

Holocausts

We frequently feel that if we expose in great detail how terrible things, such as the holocaust, have been, we will surely never allow them to occur again. History proves this is not the case. Holocausts, large and small, occur each time I judge myself, and my brother, as unworthy of being loved. Each time I want the stories we tell of hate and fear to be more real than risking to rely on that loving place we share with God, there is a cutting-off in my mind of those that God created brother to me. What ends the need for holocausts is remembering that I am wholly loved and expressing that by sharing the Presence of Love within me with everyone I meet!

To remind yourself we are all connected, when you ask for healing or the wisdom to be happy, ask it for everyone. To choose for yourself alone only ensures you will experience being alone.

Something Wrong With Us?

The ego's perception, and the world it spawns, is built upon the belief that there is something wrong with us. Every disagreement, angry thought, "natural" disaster, sickness and death, every reason not to love, arises from this single thought. All our struggles to heal disease, fix the environment, or put an end to war, has its source in this thought. Remove this thought and we are free of all its effects. Forgive this one thought when anything seems to threaten your peace and we will heal the world!

Healing of the world's every problem, every
manifestation of hate and every form of sickness,
is accomplished with a single decision: See
everyone as a part of you.

Judging God?

Today, when the first inclination to judge a brother arises in your mind, ask your God Self to show you that God, Creator of All That Is, Presence of all that is loving, is present right now in the one you are about to judge. Recognizing Him being with you now is the holy instant you have asked for. Treasure this recognition. Ask to be reminded of this moment whenever you are tempted to judge. This is the miracle of real forgiveness.

The Shortest Distance To The Truth

When looking for what is true about you, begin with acknowledging what you can depend on to be the truth: You are the wholly loving, perfectly created Child of God. Anything else is a story of what is not true. It is pointless to analyze your dreams to try to understand why you did what you seemed to do, for what you did, being only a story, is irrelevant and the "you" you look for is not there. Ask your God Self to show you how to love in every circumstance. That is the shortest distance to the truth.

Do not attempt to find the truth – until you are willing to accept the possibility that there is nothing wrong with you.

f

Practice What You Teach

What you demonstrate by the choices you make is that what you teach has value. It is your assertion of what you want. Become conscious that every choice you make impacts and influences everyone, everywhere for we are all parts of the same Self. Let the understanding of this become truth for you by consciously wanting for everyone what you would give to those you love most. And, above all, first ask what that should be.

The Peaceful Solution

A peaceful solution to any conflict is only as difficult as our willingness to forgive ourselves. When there is no need to project our own guilt, to have someone else to blame, we can want for our brother what we want for ourselves and there will be no basis for conflict of any nature. If this seems too great a stretch to believe it is only because we cannot yet imagine ourselves free of guilt.

Free The World To Love Again

If there is one thing you find unforgivable then no real forgiveness is possible for anything because you have replaced the innocence and perfection of God's Creation with a story you have made. Give every reason not to love to the One Who knows you are the very essence of what Love is and you will free the world to love again.

Deception disappears when I recognize that whatever I perceive is "wrong" comes directly from the belief there is something wrong with me.

The Buddha In Your Backyard?

Have you noticed the Buddha in your backyard? The Christ that lives just around the corner? Sometimes they are difficult to recognize because we forget it is also the Christ and the Buddha who are looking for them.

When The Moment Comes

When the moment comes that my body drops away, I want to know that I have lost no part of who I am. I want to remember the cause of my happiness is not what I do in the world. I want to know I will leave no one behind, for neither they nor I really live in the stories we tell. I want to be ready to accept that this is simply another step in the gentle "Plan" for me to remember what is true. When the moment arrives I want to trust that I am loved and merely taking another step toward home. I want to know that step is no different than the one I take today as I let go of my attachment to guilt and forgive what seems to happen here.

f

The ego prides itself on gathering as much information as it can to expand its awareness. The Voice for Truth suggests there is no particular advantage to an expanded awareness of nothing.

Connecting

Oneness is not about the "number" of God's Sons. It is about our sharing a single Source and having all the attributes that express the nature of what that Source Is. It means being connected within a single Mind with the shared intention to love.

Being Free

By not condemning what bodies do we can begin to let forgiveness teach that the body is not a part of who or what we are. By freeing our brother's body from the revenge of guilt, we free our own from the need to be sick. By not mistaking his body for who he is we are free to change the purpose for our own. By letting it become a simple tool of communication we can guarantee its perfect function in that capacity, free of sickness and "danger" of any kind.

Deception disappears when I recognize that whatever I perceive is "wrong" comes directly from the belief there is something wrong with me

Escape From Suffering Is Elusive

The reason the escape from pain and suffering seems so elusive is that we are continuously trying to correct what is wrong with us. But since there is nothing wrong with us we are actually reinforcing the dream of suffering by continuing to misperceive what is real and true. There is an error in our thinking that we must correct. The Vision our God Self holds of us does not tell us we *can* be free. It sees us free right now! Let forgiveness be the evidence of your intention to see the innocence of God's Creation, in spite of what the world would make real. Let forgiveness teach you there is peace and love where pain and suffering now seems to be. Awaken the power of your will to see what is real and true when it becomes your intention to love.

I Am Not A Body

Think of yourself without a body. It really has nothing to do with who you are and it will one day drop away. Who will you be without it? Think of those you love without a body. If you are free to simply be spirit, who could you not be with at any time? If you cannot eagerly welcome this thought you have encountered your primary obstacle to the peace and joy inherent in joining. Now would be a good time to let that go.

Neither rush to nor resist the thought of letting the body go. Focus instead on your willingness to accept everything that lives is a part of you.

You cannot remember the sensation of limitless loving while believing your mind is limited to the experience of a body.

Oneness

God did not make the world. Neither sin and guilt, nor any of its forms of pain and suffering are His Will. Everything in Creation as He knows It is a part of Him and shares His Will for perfect peace and happiness. No matter what seems real in our dream of terror, nothing stands in the way of His loving us completely. His reality is our Reality, not our dream of sin and separation. This is the awareness that heals, opening the door to a peaceful world as well as a healed body.

f

Love Defines What We Are

If you find yourself thinking about "why" you love someone, pause and realize you are vastly limiting and distorting, your true feelings for them. "Reasons" to love means there are also reasons not to love. To fully appreciate the power of your loving is to recognize there is *nothing* that can, in truth, oppose it. Thinking love has an opposite is what gives rise to all illusions. The thought of sin and separation could not exist in our awareness if we accepted this as true. If we are ever to be free of our story of sin we must be willing to love "unreasonably," for it is only love that can define what we are.

The Urge To Judge

Today, when the first inclination to judge a brother arises in your mind, ask your God Self to show you that God, Creator of All That Is, Presence of all that is loving, is present right now in the one you are about to judge. Recognizing Him being with you now is the holy instant you have asked for. Treasure this recognition. Ask to be reminded of this moment whenever you are tempted to judge. This is the miracle of real forgiveness.

Love is present whenever love looks for it.

The body is not the evidence of life. The evidence of life is the desire to love.

Our Attachment To Guilt

Letting go of our attachment to guilt is directly related to letting go of our attachment to the body, for each supports the very purpose of the other. It is therefore helpful to fully recognize the role guilt plays as resistance to our healing. Simply stated, sickness in the body is the physical manifestation of guilt in the mind. And because we believe we are a body, pain and sickness are the means we use to punish ourselves for our imagined sin. Ask God to show you the unreality of sin. Bring to mind the one whose sin is unforgivable; take his hand and ask to see his innocence. Now feel your gratitude to him for showing you your innocence that you had hidden in your judgment of him. Now notice how much "lighter," more transparent your body has become.

The Role Of Guilt

If you doubt the role guilt plays in your self-image, ask yourself if you deserve to be happy all the time. Do you always feel loved and loving towards others? Is it your natural inclination to accept someone, or to find something to criticize? If it is not normal or natural to always feel good and be loving, then some other feeling seems more important. This is the role guilt plays.

The Greatest Opportunity

The more grievous someone's behavior appears to us, the greater the urge we feel to judge. Yet this is also the greatest opportunity to release ourselves from our greatest fear. It is the one whose sin we find unforgivable who is the clearest mirror for the "reason" we cannot be freely loved. Be grateful, then, and know this brother was brought to you for your forgiveness in this most holy moment. Step back from your story of the world. For just an instant push the past aside and feel the Gift of love this Son of God can offer you. An instant will be enough, for now the fear that you are unlovable has gone.

The measure of the effectiveness of forgiveness is our ability to see our brother completely free of his story, for there is nothing there by which we can know him. Or ourselves.

You are the holiness in every holy instant.

The Dance

No one attacks another if they are at peace within themselves. Everything we "see" externally, in the world, is a mirror for the inner image we have of ourselves. Everything. By this principle then, no one is attacked by another if they are at peace within themselves. No matter how it appears we are all joined within a single consciousness, each of us responding perfectly to the beliefs that we all share. We are all part of a single consciousness. The "dance" we do together is always perfect.

When next you are tempted to judge a brother, recognize what is at stake. Know that your awakening and his are joined. What you are judging and rejecting is your best opportunity to join and be healed. Would you knowingly set your awakening aside for this?

The Mind-Body Connection

There has recently been much importance made of recognizing the "mind-body connection." Learning to "listen" to the body is thought to be important to know the body's needs. This would be true if the body had some way of communicating with us and if in fact it had needs apart from those the mind gives it. In truth, there is no consciousness in the body, no way for it to communicate with the mind. It has no feelings until they are registered by the mind. And the only needs it has are those assigned to it by the mind. The only real mind-body connection is to recognize that it is our mind that harbors the belief that we are separate and from there makes the experience of seeming to exist in a body.

The Cost of Giving

The cost of giving is receiving. You cannot give what you have not made your own. You will suffer the effects of your self-judgment, or reap the joy of your forgiveness. You will find your innocence each time your ego calls you to judge and you refuse to answer. Your experience is the perfect mirror of what you want for your brother. Refusing to judge what is not real frees you from attack. You will always teach what you want to learn. Teach only love to discover that is what you are.

Time and Space

Years ago, while contemplating a new galaxy our scientists had discovered and wondering how many more were yet to be found, I asked our Brother: How far is it to the outermost reaches of the physical universe. His answer was: *"How long does it take to think of it being there?"* A reminder that it is we who have made the world. Time, and the illusion of space it creates, is perhaps the ego's most compelling idea of proving there is something apart from and outside of us.

The saying: "I can't believe my eyes", is absolutely true.

The ego thinks free will is its ability to make infinite choices, know as much as it can, which is essential to its definition of an expanded awareness. The Voice for Truth suggests there is no particular advantage to an expanded awareness of nothing.

Love and Oneness

The nature of what love is was given us in our creation for Love is the Nature of our Creator. It cannot, therefore, be exclusive or used to set us apart. It expresses the intention of creation to infinitely extend itself knowing it will always remain the same. Love is both the essence and expression of what Oneness is. The full impact of this is realized as it satisfies its function of joining everything it touches, and touching everything it sees.

Love Without Reason

Consider this: You have never stopped being the perfect creation and extension of what God Is. There can be no guilt in you because there is no "sin" in Him. And what is true of you must be true of everyone. If you would like to experience that this is true for you, refuse to judge anyone for anything for the next hour. Give each temptation to judge to your God Self. Feel the relief that can only come with knowing that it is you who has been set free. Now feel the joy that comes with knowing you are free to love for no reason at all.

When you have trouble "hearing" guidance from the God Self, remember, only when you are willing to be loved are you available to hear the Voice that speaks of love.

Your Holy Self

There is a place in you where everything you want to know is known; where you are complete and whole. It is a place where every moment is filled with joy and nothing interrupts loving. There is nothing you need to learn to find this place; it always has been yours. It only hides behind a thought that something else is true, some reason that you cannot be loved. One wholly untrue thought, made real by lifetimes of pain and suffering. Decide today you are willing to be shown this thought is false and the awareness of your holy Self, will spring to life and lead you there.

We All Want The Same Thing

What does our brother or our sister really want of us? It's easy to be deceived. But no matter how it looks, you will find it is exactly what you want of them. We have tried to project our self-guilt onto them to make them "worse" than we. And they have done the same. But when we realize we both want the same thing - to know that we are loved - we can find that love within ourselves and gladly give it to join with them.

Without The Fear Of Death

Without the fear of death the Love of God is instantly remembered. It is the belief in death that is the egos "proof" our guilt is real and death becomes the answer to "God's demand" for atonement. Understanding this, we can see where the ego's fear of God comes from and why it feels a need to maintain a sense of separateness from Him. In truth, it is only our guilt we fear, but each judgment we make of one another to satisfy that guilt becomes another layer of fear separating us from "deserving" to be loved ourselves. Lets agree to forgive our guilt and the need to die and join in our willingness to accept the Love God offers. Lets accept Gods gift of life for everyone who now think that they must die.

Where Love Is Free To find Itself

Many resist the notion that we are all awakening together, but it cannot be otherwise if God has only one Son. To deny our own readiness we say there are others not ready to awaken. What seems to be "those" ready and not ready to awaken is the one, but fractured, ego consciousness wrestling with the need to be separate. When that need is gone what was thought of as many will be recognized as the multi-faceted one. Now the purpose of the world will change. A new world that welcomes Heaven will then arise, and love will be free to find itself.

How do you accept yourself unconditionally? For an instant, see yourself without a past; without your story of the world. Just that. No history, no guilt; no reason not to be loved.

Accept yourself unconditionally and you will recognize that everyone is part of you.

Accept yourself unconditionally and there will be no one you do not love.

f

Our Mirror of Love

The world is a reflection of how we see ourselves. It can be a peaceful experience or an endless variety of threats. In effect this means that our behavior is based upon what we believe is true about us. If we feel badly about ourselves we will behave in a way that is unacceptable to others. But by discovering there is a way to find a different and a loving self, we will then present a loving self to the world and find a loving world in return.

Intentionally Connecting

The best way to convince yourself that your experience is what you want it to be, is to create situations intentionally. Before attending your next function decide on the outcome you will have from meeting someone there. Pay particular attention to how others play their part to accomplish "your" chosen goal. Remember this when you are tempted to feel victimized by your brother's choices. We are one in both truth and illusion.

The Means to Remember Heaven

We have been given the means to remember Heaven. It is with the vision the God Self holds for us and comes to us through the practice of forgiveness. It is simple and direct and unfolds as we hear Him say: *There is no sin in Heaven for there is no desire not to Love.* Outside our story of the world, there is no sin in our brother for God's Love is still present there. In him is Heaven where both of us remain. But when you see sin in him the Vision of Heaven is lost. Forgive him. Free him of your guilty projections. Ask your God Self to see and embrace your connection to him and in your joining will the awareness of Heaven return to both of you.

Sacrifice

When seen through the ego's belief, the thought of letting the world go appears to be sacrificing what sustains us and all that we can clearly relate to. Yet what we are learning through the forgiving process will teach us that it is not the world that is the cause of our experience; it is our thoughts of what we think is true about us. And when we have discovered it is only our thoughts that bring us peace and make us safe and happy, we will not need to judge or look to the world for what has never been there anyway. Now, recognizing its source, we are free to change that world.

Sacrifice is the price of guilt. Deprivation is the justification of attack. Forgiveness is the choice to see another reality and let love solve your problems.

For years I prided myself on being a good problem solver. Then I began to notice how regularly I had problems to solve.

Are You Ready?

Receiving guidance you cannot "hear" and letting it bring peace and joy to your life seems an impossible conundrum. In fact, it is not necessary to hear or understand your guidance to have it change your life. What is necessary is that you want your life to change and you are willing to let go the beliefs that make it what it now seems to be. This is difficult because to the ego understanding is a prerequisite to trust. If you could accept, however, that a path is now laid out for you to follow, the only choice you would need to make is whether or not you are ready to follow it.

Who Is In Charge?

It is significant to note, when you have chosen to let your God Self make your choices for you and something unloving shows up, you have allowed your ego back in control and it is time to choose again. You may be certain this is not something the God Self has planned. It does not teach through sacrifice or pain. It is simply not confused about what is real and what is just a dream.

The Justification For forgiveness

Our attempts to make real what God did not create is the cause of all our pain and turmoil. All our learning hinges on our willingness to let go of a story that is not true. Recognizing the difference between truth and illusion is a choice our God Self will make for us, if we allow it. It is also the choice between peace and conflict, joy and fear. It is the one real justification of forgiveness. It is what gives us the freedom to remember we are loved.

Two Kinds Of Choices

There are two kinds of choices we can make: Those in alignment with our ego belief, or those that can change it; those that promote the world as we now see it, or those that lead to a more peaceful and loving world. Choices always reflect the belief they come from. Don't delude yourself about what your belief is and think you can "blend" the choices. If you are committed to choosing what is real, ask your God Self to choose for you. It is possible to abandon ourselves to the truth.

When you have let go the thought of sin, there will be nothing in your mind to prevent you from being wholly joyful and loving every one you see.

Giving and Receiving Are The Same

The awareness that giving and receiving are the same is essential in recognizing how we make our world and how we can change it. Our thoughts are both the cause and the effect of our experience. Choose to judge your brother and you will suffer the unhappiness and pain of what you judged him for. Forgive and choose to love him and you will feel all the joy that being loved can bring. The one you would condemn or love is part of you. As you forgive him, you learn to love yourself.

Rumi

It is difficult for us to practice forgiveness while using the ego's perception to decide where it is needed. In ACIM Jesus tells us that nothing we now see in the world is true. He summarizes the purpose of what ACIM teaches this way: "Nothing real can be threatened. Nothing unreal exists. Herein lies the peace of God." Throughout our history many wise teachers have echoed the same thought. Eight hundred years ago Rumi expressed it like this: *"Out beyond ideas of wrong doing and right doing, there is a field. I will meet you there."*

Gifts of forgiveness

Every gift of forgiveness given to another is returned to you. Every "sin" of theirs you refuse to acknowledge as real, frees you from its fearful consequences. And every reason not to love that you choose to disavow brings you closer to the Source of Love. Our thoughts express what we want for ourselves, so ask that they come from the place in you that wants only love. Affirm that this is all you want by not judging what is not loving, because not being the creation of God, it cannot be real.

Nothing Real Can Be Threatened

Early on in my experience with Jesus' presence, I was expressing my self-judgment and disappointment about how I so frequently found myself returning to my ego judgments. He listened patiently , then said, "It would be helpful to remember that in your thought process you have only two choices. You will either experience the Peace and Love of God, or nothing is happening. In neither case is judgment or disappointment justified." Another succinct reminder. "Nothing real can be threatened. Nothing unreal exists."

When you have trouble "hearing" guidance from the God Self, remember, only when you are willing to be loved are you available to hear the Voice that speaks of love.

What Do We Accept As Real and True?

What we see inside is what makes the world we see outside. What is true for us inside becomes real in our world. This means that what affects us is not a matter of how we react to what we see. That is only the trick of projection our perception uses to confirm what it has already decided is true. What affects us then is what we decide is real and true. We must remember this when deciding what kind of reality we give to the thoughts we choose to accept as true.

Accept that God created you as the Presence of Love and make His Love real in your world.

The Purpose Of A Holy Instant

The purpose of a holy instant is to show you that everything you pursue exists in you right now. There is no past or future. There is only the infinite now. There is no future moment you will awaken to the truth. When your innocence has been accepted you will recognize it always has been 'now.' The "value" of remembering the past ensures we will retain the pain of judgments made today. How do we let the past go? Judge nothing today that has its origin there. In other words, judge nothing today.

f

The Risk Of Surrendering To Love

When it becomes apparent that nothing comes to us but by our will, do we become aware of our attachment to the world that we have made. Ask yourself simply if what you want is Heaven or your idealized version of a perfect world. Would you have God's creation, or what the ego has made? It is our desire to "improve" and keep what we have that prevents our mind from accepting the wonders of all that awaits us just past the veil of our perception that sin is real. Ask today that your illusions be forgiven. Run the risk of surrendering to Love.

The Fear Of Pain And Death

The fear of pain and death is the direct effect of our self-imposed guilt. And we increase its strength and hold over us with every judgment of our brother's "guilt." Love is the antidote for fear, but love cannot be found where guilt is perceived to be. It is also true that sin cannot exist where there is love. We only need to choose for love because we have forgotten love is what we are. But if fear is what we want we must choose that as well, otherwise it could not exist. Forgive your guilt, the cause of fear; declare that sin is not real. The opposition to love will now be gone and without its cause the idea of pain and death will disappear.

A Reminder

Periodically I must remind myself there is never more than a single issue for me to face: Is sin real? It is from this belief that all my misperceptions arise. When I know, when I really believe sin is not real, my sense of separateness, every appearance that there is a lack of love, my pain and suffering and all the rest of my dreaming will be finished. Then too, I must also remember why forgiveness is the most powerful of all our illusions. It is the one that will end the others for all time.

The Vision Of Holiness

Truth is always with you. Learn to depend on that. The Vision of holiness has never left your mind. To see your brother sinless requires that you want to use this Vision more than your perception of your sinfulness that now hides this truth from you. Our entire perception arises from the belief there is something wrong with us. But if we want to forgive we can let go of judgment and make acceptance our priority. We can exercise our Vision of holiness and create a habit of seeing what is right, instead of what is wrong. We can make the space for a loving world to be born into our consciousness.

forgiving Thoughts

It is our thoughts that make the world we now see. Coming from the belief in sin, they are ultimately all thoughts of death. If you have any doubt about this, try to find something in the physical world that does not "die." The next time you find yourself wondering if you can forgive something terrible that has happened in this world, remember the kind of thinking that has made it a place where "terrible" can happen. Imagine now what kind of world loving thoughts could make and feel the difference forgiveness will bring.

To end the fear of death stop resisting the life you share with your brother.

f

We Are Where God Is

You could only be a body living in a world, if God were a body and living there too. For you are a part of Him and like Him in every way. Lets all stop pretending to be an ego. It is not a role we were meant to play.

f

Responsibility For My Thoughts

I am only free to change the self I have made and the world it sees when I have claimed full responsibility for having made them. And I am only free to want something different when I admit I do not know what I really want. This acknowledgment alone will open my mind to the Presence of the Gift God has placed there. Relying upon that Presence and experiencing the joy that comes with It shows me what I really want and allows me to shift my faith from fear to love. Now I am free to see you sinless and sharing a world of peace with me.

You Are Not A Body

Recognizing our innocence is a prerequisite to our awakening to the truth. To recognize how resistant we are to accepting the truth we have to face how attached we are to our primary illusion – the belief we are a body. It is impossible to accept innocence while believing that what we are is the very thing that symbolizes our guilt. Then I must ask: If the body is not real and I am committed not to judge what is not real, can I justify judging what a "body" might do? In short, it is not possible to see the truth while thinking the body plays some role in who we are.

The World Will Not Bring Us Peace

We sometimes think there are things and experiences in the world that bring us peace and joy. We forget it is we who made the world. We must be reminded that the "default" condition of our mind is perfect peace and infinite happiness. Before we introduced the idea of guilt and all that it entails, there was nothing to interrupt the awareness of loving and being loved. Rather than looking, then, for reasons to forgive what has happened in the world, ask simply to share the Vision our God Self holds of who we were before we imagined that the thought of sin could take the place of Love. Now we have a peaceful vision of our Self that we can offer to the world.

Refuse to judge what isn't real and be free to find your real Self.

Victim and Victimizer Are Joined

Events that involve great suffering present the most difficult challenge not to judge. Often it feels to the ego that not to condemn is not to care. Yet if inflicting senseless suffering on one another is ever to cease, victim and victimizer must be joined in the awareness that their "sin" is not real; that their need to punish or be punished, is self-inflicted. Both share the same guilt and are healed together or not at all. We must be able to see that all our stories are the same and are equally untrue if we are to love everyone equally as part of who we are. Our heart is open to both or closed to both, for fear and love cannot co-exist. To every story of sin and suffering our response must always be the same. I will not judge it because it is not the thought of God and so cannot be real.

"Proof" That Sin Is Real

Look outward at the world and you will see the "proof" that sin is real and every living thing is different from all the others. This is not the Thought of God that extends Itself, infinitely ensuring that everything be like Itself. Look within if you would find this Thought. It surely must be there for It is What you are. And when you find it there, a sinless "real" world will unfold to replace the one you now see. You will then recognize it has always been right there within your mind and part of you. What in one moment had seemed like hell is now recognized as Heaven and you will know you are at Home.

Finding YourSelf

You may think your journey to the truth is a path you have followed alone, but In Truth that would be impossible because we all are parts of a single, interwoven consciousness. Where one goes, all must surely go. Only in this story of separate bodies doing different things at different times will it seem that one could go ahead while another is holding back. But different stories cannot make different what really is the same. For a moment, remove your brother from his story. Wipe away every trace of what he did or did not do. Leave nothing in your mind by which he could be judged. Here you are free of both his story *and yours*. In this moment of innocence you are joined and here you recognize that you have found your Self.

Trying To Bring Light To Darkness

When sin is even subtly real in our belief, it seems a natural thing to atone in some way for what we perceive we have done. It is a popular belief that there are those already enlightened who will incarnate to be the victim of unloving acts to demonstrate, for example, their willingness to suffer pain or die to prove death is unreal. But one who knew we cannot die would recognize that sin is the cause of deaths misperception and through forgiveness teach it is sin that is unreal. We have many ways of trying to bring light to the darkness, wanting to make our perception real. It is good to remember the Holy Spirit's Plan never involves sacrifice or suffering.

f

Perfect Love

When someone speaks to you of their belief in guilt and fear, don't be tempted to correct them with "better information." Recognize instead that the cause of their fear is founded in a belief there is something wrong with them that prevents their being loved. On their own behalf, forgive them. Bring forth the Presence of our one God Self and hold them in the Vision of His perfect Love. Feel the oneness that bonds you with them in that Love. And then be grateful for the opportunity given you by them to heal your own guilt and fear.

How Far Is Heaven?

How far away is Heaven? Take someone's hand and together proclaim, "There is no guilt in us for there is none in God. We will accept no thought that would make us different from each other or from our one Source." Then together reach out your hand and take God's Hand that welcomes you home. In this moment you realize that only Love is real and recognize you are in Heaven now, for there is no other place to be.

f

Sin Denies The Reality Of Love

Sin denies the reality of love. Real forgiveness denies the reality of sin. Therefore, real forgiveness always results in loving. There is no thought but sin, which so effectively hides the Presence of Love. But the most important aspect of loving is that it only comes when there is no cost for it. It is, in fact, already present in our mind, hidden behind the self-judgments we make. So let the temptation to judge become a reminder to forgive, and remove the only block there is to remembering that you are wholly loved.

Love seems to be elusive when finding guilt is important.

To Love Is Natural

To love is the most basic, natural instinct we have. Its purpose is to infinitely extend and embrace all that it encounters in order that it forever remain what It Is. We cannot stop the desire to love, it has no opposite. But we can disassociate from our real, loving Self. Guilt is the cause of our Self-denial. Forgiveness teaches us to overlook what is not real. Choose to see your brother's sinless and experience the joy of joyning.

Your Natural Desire To Love

We try to deflect our guilt by judging others for what we think is wrong with us. Needing others to judge is the purpose for separateness and the only reason there seems to be a world "outside" of us. This is the reason projection seems possible; the one mad thought that could seem to fragment what is complete and whole. Forgive the world madness has made by judging nothing that happens there. Ask your God Self to show you the innocent brother that lives inside your mind. Then feel your natural desire to love him when unencumbered by what your outside world has seemed to make of him.

See A Sinless World

Is it your purpose to embrace the truth? Each time we turn to something other than love to answer a dispute we have diminished and distorted loves purpose. When we look to something in the world to bring us peace or make us happy we have denied where the Source of peace and happiness is. Look back upon your day and count the times you have attacked the truth. You strengthen your belief in what you perceive is true by what you practice. Decide to make no judgments before you clarify your intention to love. When you see a sinless world you will know you have embraced the truth.

See Your Brother Sinless

When you see less than perfect loving in your brother it is because you do not see him at all. You see an illusion of him mirroring an illusion of yourself. If you would find the truth of yourself you must not think that the story he tells of his illusion is real. Whether in truth or illusion, you will think you both are the same. You can choose to either love him for who he really is, or hate him because his story seems different from yours. Either way, what you think is true of him is now charting the course of your life experience.

"Where" Is The Real World?

Where is the real world? The one where peace and joy and love exist eternally? It is here, surrounding us right now, waiting only to be seen. The world we see instead is but a story we tell of pain and divisiveness because that is what we expect from a story authored by the illusion of sin. But the author of this story lives only in the story. We can now choose to let forgiveness end this chapter and let God's Innocence unfold a peaceful story of joy and love. Which story we choose will depend on what we want to find. Lets choose to look for a sinless world whose innocence will mirror our own and open our hearts to love.

You Are The Love Of God

You are the presence, the expression and the experience of the Love of God. You are the guarantee of eternal life and co-creator of All That Is. Nothing lives but lives in you. And you are one with every aspect of creation. It is impossible that anything exist that lacks anything that exists. Remember this when something seems missing from your life. Remind yourself that this is as true now as it will ever be true. And most of all remember, nothing hides this truth from us but the thought of sin. Forgive your brother's story. Restore the innocence of God's Creation in the only place that it is missing: In your awareness.

Our Purpose Is Joined

Having a special, unique or different purpose to save the world is the ego's favorite way to maintain the value of being different and separate. You can be absolutely certain if you perceive your function can set you apart, the world you save will remain apart from truth.

Love is present everywhere, but only recognized by love itself. Joy is found instantly in the choice to be joyful. And peace is never found in conflict. To know yourself recognize everything as part of you. See your purpose and mine joined in a single goal: To recognize the face of God in everyone.

Would you like to be free of conflict and welcome peace into your life, giving it a home where anyone can come to heal and to rest? We all can do this simply by refusing to attack the Self that is God's one Son.

It is Not You Who Suffers Pain

When pain or doubt, fear or confusion, seems to control your thinking, remind yourself it is not you who suffers pain or is in fear. It is impossible that you have ever stopped being what you were created to be. Your awareness of who you are has momentarily left you. It is now the ego made image of a guilty and isolated self that fills your mind and wants to suffer. But mind will serve the purpose that you give it and there is another Presence there Whose purpose is to end your pain, to forgive every illusion present there. Call upon this Self that knows you cannot suffer or be confused. Let go the feeling that you need to be deserving of it and simply be willing to accept the miracle of real forgiveness. Now it can be yours.

f

The Ego Is An Idea Of Guilt

The ego is nothing more than an idea of guilt in the mind of the innocent Child of God. No experience that has arisen from that guilty thought, be it of hatred, murder, pain or death has touched or changed the innocence of that child as God created It. Nothing that is real has changed. Only the awareness of the ego's consciousness has been affected. And though many things seem to have changed in the ego's world, that is not where the holy Child lives.

Claim Your Truthful Place

When you are caught in a situation so overcome with fear and hate that forgiveness seems impossible, remember that it is only your thoughts of fear and hate that are the cause of what you feel. They are not the truth. Remember too that you are the determiner of the direction our consciousness will choose to go; of the beliefs it will bring to the world. As you decide whether to forgive or to condemn, consider the kind of world you want for those you love. Do not dismiss your presence as a grain of sand upon the beach of time. That could only be true if we did not share the Will of God. Claim your truthful place as the undivided Presence of God and choose for love instead of fear.

Would it change our need to be separate and different, if what we wanted for our brother was for him to feel perfectly loved? Especially knowing that what we want for him is what we make true for ourselves?

Love Surrounds Us

All around us there is only love, when we have eyes to see it. Don't be discouraged if you cannot see or feel it yet. Our ego need to keep its guilt still seems strong, seeming even to strengthen as we move closer to our goal. Our inclination is to intensify our efforts to move past these feelings, to resist our resistance to surrender. And because our resistance only strengthens what we resist, disappointment sets in. Focus instead on the one thing we do not resist: The desire to be loved. This desire will find the Place in us it is fulfilled, for we have asked to recognize our will and God's are one. Now we can move past the belief our guilt is real, to the place love holds for us.

Would it change our need to be separate and different, if what we wanted for our brother was for him to be perfectly loved? Especially knowing that what we want for him is what we make true for ourselves?

If you would see your brother change, change what you think is true about him.

The Separation

There is a thought within our consciousness that we have sinned and lost our connection to Love. Believing this to be true we have made a part of our self to take the blame, separated from that part and now call it "brother." But our efforts at projection have not been entirely effective. The idea that we are guilty still remains with us. We call that idea, "ego." And as we respond to the ego idea that we are bad by judging our "brother" for it, we have come to accept that this ego is who we are. Whether we see it as a brother or an ego, the idea has become a real entity. And thinking of it being some-thing other than an idea, makes letting it go infinitely harder. Reduce sin to what it really is – an idea that would substitute the power of hate for love. Now decide if that "idea" is what you want.

Choose to see your brother's innocence and experience the joy of joyning.

Find Your Holiness

The world you see, and so your life experience, is bound by how you see the one you judge most harshly. This is true because that one represents the deepest fears about yourself. It must also be true then, that to find the holiness of this one reveals the loving presence you thought that you had lost. Forgiveness is the way you find his holiness, and yours. What is true of him must be true of you, for neither of us has escaped the Mind of God.

Every judgment I make of you reasserts there is something wrong with me. The fundamental law of perception depends upon projection.

What Do You Want From Life?

What do you want from life? What kind of world do you want to see? Think about this for a while, and then ask another question. What are you willing to bring to life? What kind of world do you support with the choices you make? We are only afraid of being responsible for the world we see when we feel powerless to change it.

Beyond The Body

To find yourself you must be willing to find what lives beyond the body, for there is nothing about the body that can speak of what is true about you. Only your willingness to use the body to communicate with other bodies can be a useful purpose for it. And only when you communicate the innocence of love do you communicate what will lead you to the truth. I ask today to know that only love is real. I will not judge what seems unloving and so try to make not loving seem real.

Perception vs. Truth

It is important for us to recognize what our perception is and how it works so that we don't confuse it with the truth. Perception is a way of thinking needed to support and validate our belief that there is something wrong with us, and everyone else as well. It then judges everything its thoughts have made, denying responsibility for what happens by projecting the cause of everything it has imagined onto a world it has made for just this purpose. Thanks to God there is an alternative to this insanity. His Answer is with us now, waiting for the moment we decide to turn to Him. Ask for help, then watch for someone to appear who also needs help. Ask how you can help him. This will change entirely the purpose of a perception previously used only to find fault. Give him what you both want and find the bond that has always existed between you. Now we become aware there really is another way to see, a different world to be seen.

free of perception there is no reason not to love. Without a reason not to love you will find your real, loving Self.

End Suffering

Would you like to end suffering in the world? If so, you must first see that suffering is not real. It is not real because its cause — sin — is not real. Sin is not real because it would confirm that something could exist that would oppose the Love of God. Remember, when you judge anything it is because you believe it will affect you. You then have made it real and imposed its effects upon the world you see. Would you end suffering in the world? Then see the one who suffers free of sin.

If *forgiving* someone does not reveal that you are free of guilt, keep at it.

The belief in sin empowers hate; guilt's behavior justifies it. Forgiveness asserts, "it didn't happen," turns it all to smoke and gently blows it away.

What Do You Really Want?

We do not now recognize that what we really want is what we already have until we begin to consciously take responsibility for our thoughts. The way we learn this is to practice expressing a different standard of what we want to be true by the choices we make. This is the purpose of forgiveness; consciously choosing to recognize that it is love we want to find, not guilt, and so make choices inspired by our desire to love instead of the ego's need to look for fault.

Do This One Thing

Do this one thing and you will change the purpose of your perception from looking for fear to finding love. Be willing to consider there is no reason for you to resist the Love of God. Do this by joining with your brother, the Means God has chosen for sharing love with you. Do not accept perception's judgment of what it sees your brother do for it does not recognize the love in either of you.

Judgment and condemnation support a perception that something is wrong. Forgiveness supports a perception that there is no opposite to love. The perception you choose to support becomes the world you see.

139

Love's Purpose

We cannot be too often reminded that the world we see is not a place. It is literally a state of mind, made by the perception that sees it; a perception that sees only what confirms what it already believes. This is not different in principle from God's Law that Love recreates Itself by seeing only What It Is. The purpose of the ego's perception is to look for what is wrong for that expresses its belief. Love's purpose is to find love for that is all it knows. In the ego's search to find what is wrong it has lost the meaning of what love is and where it can be found. This can be reversed by deciding to look for love. Ask to see the holiness in every brother. Change what you want your perception to find and your perception will change that you may find it.

Every judgment I make of you reasserts there is something wrong with me. The fundamental law of perception depends upon projection.

Your Wholly Loving Self

What does it really mean that your brother is a part of you? To the ego, used to functioning alone, it has no meaning. In truth, however, it means you cannot completely fulfill any function without him. You cannot love totally, be completely happy or fully at peace, without him. You cannot wholly make a choice that excludes him. You cannot in any meaningful way begin to know the truth about yourself without knowing the same is true of him. As we are the Will of God we are also the Will of one another. But to know this Will, to know this Self, it must be recognized as undivided. When you next are tempted to be different or stand apart, remind yourself, you must be willing to let go of your separateness if you are ever to find your wholly loving Self.

Are you available to make choices in this "now" moment that will bring you greater peace and joy? You may answer "yes" to this only if you have forgiven everything you once valued from the past.

Who You Are

Who you are is an experience of what you think, not what you do. And it is the intention you have for your thoughts that determines the outcome you will have from them. This is true both of perception and of knowing, because it is spirit / thought that constitutes the infinite nature of our Being. The body plays no part in who we are. It can only seem to be "where" we are because of the part it plays in the story of separateness we are telling. When we decide there is nothing wrong with our real self we will let the body go. Free then of the story we will find the ones we are joined with in love where we all, always have been: Here in this infinitely present now moment. The myth of separation will be done.

In a world made of conflict and contradictions
there is one thing you absolutely can depend on:
Everyone wants to know they are loved, and
capable of loving. Depend on this when you are
tempted to see differences between you and your
brother.

To avoid surprises in any situation, you need only
be clear about what kind of outcome you wanted
from it.

Intention = Outcome

Learning that perception only shows you what you want to see, that your intention for something determines the outcome of your experience of it, demonstrates that cause and effect are always together, cannot be separated. While this teaches us that we can choose to have a more peaceful and happy life, the greater learning is that we have never separated from our Cause. We are the Effect of God and a part of all He has created. There is no reality – no life – apart from His. This knowing of our oneness will, when fully grasped, bring all illusions to an end.

All The Joy Of Heaven

If you knew that your mind, right now, held all the peace and joy of heaven, would you open your mind to share it with everyone? If you knew all the Love of God was yours to give, would you give it to everyone? If you knew that you could end all the worlds hunger and pain and suffering of every nature, would you do it? Then know these are the choices you make with each decision to judge or to forgive, for all of Heaven, all God's Love is in you now waiting only to be shared. The world is ours to heal.

When you have let go the thought of sin, there will be nothing in your mind to prevent you from being wholly joyful and loving every one you see.

Love Lifts Every Burden

Guilt, expressed as hatred, puts a terrible burden on the mind. If you doubt this, look at the pain and suffering found in the world that guilt has made. Love, on the other hand, lifts every burden from our mind. Judgment divides mind, limiting its awareness of what it is. Love frees it to the perfect harmony that comes with acceptance of our whole Self. Take a few minutes every day to free your mind of the burdens that are there. Without a specific focus, ask simply to feel only loves Presence. When you feel the literal weight that is lifted from you, you will recognize how we so "naturally" abuse ourselves with our judgments, even when they seem intended for others. It will become apparent who first benefits from your forgiveness.

Give your perception a different purpose. Let it now be the means for returning to your brother the love he thought he had lost.

"Moving mountains" is easier when you know what they are made of and who made them.

All The Joy Of Heaven

If you knew that your mind, right now, held all the peace and joy of heaven, would you open your mind to share it with everyone? If you knew all the Love of God was yours to give, would you give it to everyone? If you knew that you could end all the worlds hunger and pain and suffering of every nature, would you do it? Then know these are the choices you make with each decision to judge or to forgive, for all of Heaven, all God's Love is in you now waiting only to be shared. The world is ours to heal.

If we are finally to find peace and be free of fear, faith in each other is not an option.

To learn to love yourself, find no reason to judge your brother.

Perception of Others

What is perhaps the hardest thing for us to recognize and then accept is that what seems to be our perception of others is not about them at all. Yet, correspondingly, we are so accustomed to projecting our self-criticism onto them, it is through recognizing what we judge them for that we learn why we judge ourselves. This is why we are encouraged to "see our brother's holiness," for that is where we have hidden our own. The discovery, then, of finding them together confirms the recognition of our Self as whole and undivided.

Remember, every time you condemn your brother or yourself, you condemn the One Who has created both of you just like Himself.

How Does God See You?

The way you see your brother mirrors the way you think God sees you. Your every judgment of him reflects what you believe is due you. You will suffer your condemnation of him because it is, in truth, your judgment of yourself. But if you allow the God Self to show you your brother's holiness, in that awareness of him you will find God's Love for you. The path to Heaven cannot be walked alone.

When someone speaks to you of their belief in guilt and fear, don't be tempted to correct them with "better information." Recognize instead that the cause of their fear is founded in a belief there is something wrong with them that prevents their being loved. On their own behalf, forgive them. Bring forth the Presence of our one God Self and hold them in the Vision of His perfect Love. Feel the oneness that bonds you with them in that Love. And then be grateful for the opportunity given you by them to heal your own guilt and fear.

Creation is the extension of Its Creator and exists only in His Mind. When you are tempted to judge someone, reflect for a moment on What you are judging and Who you share this mind with.

The Dualistic Mind

Our mind, as we now experience it, is divided between ego perception and God Self knowing. Perception's belief is that sin is real and results in the experience of separation and conflict. Knowing sees all of life connected, resulting in peace and harmony. Knowledge is there permanently because the Mind was founded in Truth by the Creator of Truth for the purpose of preserving and extending what is True. Perception is there because we have tried to make a different "truth." It is not permanent and must be continuously chosen to maintain its presence. Judgment of what is "wrong" exercises the choice for perception. Forgiveness makes no judgment and frees the mind to see from its natural, peaceful state. Which we choose determines the future of the world we see.

Creation is the extension of Its Creator and exists only in His Mind. When you are tempted to judge someone, reflect for a moment on What you are judging and Who shares this mind with you.

Knowing The Love of God

If you would know the Love of God then you must forgive everything you now see. It is not the function of perception to show you what is true. Its sole purpose is to confirm what you already believe; to support an image of yourself that is not loved. But love is present in your mind where something else is now perceived. Withdraw your judgments of what you see and you must find the Love of God is there because, in truth, nothing else really can be.

Seeing Differently

You cannot judge your your brother by what you see in the world and recognize his holiness. You cannot in any way identify him with the character in his story and find his truth. How then, while the world still seems real, can we transcend what our perception insists is true? Two things make it possible: The Presence of our God Self to take the place of our perception, and the power of our desire to see differently. Exercise your power to accept God's Vision. Ask to see your brother's holiness and find his truth and yours together, where it has always been.

To learn to love yourself, find no reason to judge
your brother.

Your Natural Desire To Love

We try to deflect our guilt by judging others for what we think is wrong with us. Needing others to judge is the purpose for separateness and the only reason there seems to be a world "outside" of us. This is the reason projection seems possible; the one mad thought that could seem to fragment what is complete and whole. Forgive the world madness has made by judging nothing that happens there. Ask your God Self to show you the innocent brother that lives inside your mind. Then feel your natural desire to love him when unencumbered by what your outside world has seemed to make of him.

Choose for God Who knows only Love and Love must surely find you, for you have chosen what you already are.

The Choice To Awaken

One of the few choices we cannot make is whether to live or die. Neither can we choose to love or not to love. We can choose to keep or let go the physical symbol of our separateness. We can choose to awaken to our awareness of Loves Presence, or continue to ignore it is within us. We can, in short, experience the effects of our belief. We can even deny the truth. But we cannot change it. So relax. Truth is always present, whether we seem to be, or not.

Freedom is the experience of feeling no need to judge anything. Perpetual forgiveness will get you there.

There is a state of mind from which only happy thoughts arise. It is where two have consciously chosen to see they are the same. Without differences all sense of conflict is gone. And with harmony is happiness found, for now there is nothing to block the natural flow of loving.

A Thought Of Separateness

Your mind is not a part of, or attached to, your body. Yet there is a thought of separateness within our mind and that is what is experienced as a body. What "shapes" the thought that seems to be a body, what determines its size, whether it is sick or what its limits are, is a function of the purpose we have for this "self" we have made. Believe that there is something wrong with you and the body will pay the price you think appropriate for that "sin." But if you see yourself as harmless with no need to harm, you will be free of harm's effects. And should you elect to let love guide you, then whatever your body seems to do or say will communicate love's message to everyone.

The belief in sin empowers hate; guilt's behavior justifies it. Forgiveness asserts, "it only happened in your story," turns it all to smoke and gently blows it away.

We are not the characters in a story of sin. We are the adventure of loving.

f

A World That Love Has Made

I feel the strength of my desire to let the world of pain and suffering go. But there are moments I also feel the appeal this world has as "home" to those I dearly love. I ask Brother how to see this. He says,

"Value the world as a learning experience to tell the difference between what is real and what is only your ego's perception. What you will learn is that only love is real and as you see the lack of love in the perception that has made this world, you become more receptive to a world that love has made, allowing that world to then appear. In this way you do not create the need to abandon what has familiar appeal to you until you have made a "real" substitute you value even more. Soon then, all the attributes of separation will lose their appeal and drop away. But the transition has been made with no sense of loss by simply letting love do what it must always do: unite you with your whole and real Self."

Surrendering Our Perception

We have each used the judgments of our perception that there is something wrong with us to make an image of a self, a brother and a world. Each of these images seems to be unique and different, creating different reasons why the world is real. We are in the process of surrendering that perception to the truth. But because it has created a belief that we are different with separate minds, we do not yet see all stories are the same or that we share a single consciousness and Mind. From the perspective of our separateness, then, it would seem we each must let our separate perception go. It is to this end we each have a "special" function in the world. It is to forgive our particular version why sin is real. It is to find our brother's holiness, just past the images we have imposed and find the loving self we have hidden there.

You could only be a body living in a world if God were a body and living there too. For you are a part of Him and like Him in every way. Let's all stop pretending to be an ego. It is not a role we were meant to play.

Special Function

Our special function in the world is inevitably entwined with those we are close to. Consciously or unconsciously we engage in the awakening process with those perceptions that parallel our own. It will not be an accident to witness either your belief, or what seems to be its opposite, in those you regularly associate with. Be mindful then of the opportunity love is offering you. No matter how you perceived it, the purpose of every special function is, first, to recognize and then to nurture, Love's Presence. It is also good to remember that all encounters happen because in that moment it is they that bear the greatest potential for bringing you to the truth.

God's Purpose For Us

Everything must fulfill its purpose. Such is the nature of belief. We seem to have conflicting purposes now. The ego's purpose is to prove sin real; to make a world of attack and suffering where everything must die. God's Purpose for us is an extension of His Own; to love without exception and beyond the limits of time. Forgiveness is your acknowledgment you accept God's Purpose as your own.

Feeling His Love reflected everywhere then changes this world's purpose for everyone, and for all time.

Undeserving Thoughts

We are Beings of spirit / mind. Our experience is determined by our thoughts and the meaning we give them. When we do not question what we deserve, we are free to have what we want. This is particularly true as it concerns our desire to be loved. Forgive your brother his every undeserving thought and discover how loved you really are.

The Need To Love

The ego professes many needs, but in truth has only one: The need to love. It is the need it must deny, frequently tucking it just behind its desire to be loved; another feeling it must hide. The need to love arises from our function as a co-creator; to extend what Love Is. Seen through the ego's perception of its guilt, the drive to be loving is often confused with the feeling we are unlovable. This confusion can be clarified with a simple, though not easy, illustration. When next you feel unloved, ask to have someone brought to you who needs assurance they are loved. Now ask your God Self to exercise your natural desire to love them. Do this and you will end all confusion that there is a difference between loving and being loved.

Changing The World

Is it the world we need to change, or the mind that made it? We believe it is the world because we think it is the world that shapes our experience. Watching the world change as we change our thoughts demonstrates the truer lesson, that it is our thoughts that shape our experience. Forgiveness is one of the best illustrations we have of this. Condemn someone and the world will show you their attack. Forgive that same person with the intention to love them and you will find a brother. Which world will you choose?

Finding YourSelf

You may think your journey to the truth is a path you have followed alone, but In Truth that would be impossible because we all are parts of a single, interwoven consciousness. Where one goes, all must surely go. Only in this story of separate bodies doing different things at different times will it seem that one could go ahead while another is holding back. But different stories cannot make different what really is the same. For a moment, remove your brother from his story. Wipe away every trace of what he did or did not do. Leave nothing in your mind by which he could be judged. Here you are free of both his story *and yours*. In this moment of innocence you are joined and here you recognize that you have found your Self.

The Holy Child Of God

Can you forgive a serial killer, a terrorist or child molester? Probably not. For once you have identified them as such you have set them apart from you and made real both their crime and the one you have judged yourself for. The way you define a person or situation unconsciously sets your expectation from it. Forgiveness is more than a release from guilt. It is the reminder that what we judge has no reality beyond the story our perception has made. Ask instead if you can forgive the Holy Child of God masquerading as one of the world's best storytellers. Redefining your thoughts will help you to see differently.

The "Cost" of Love

No one will gain if anyone can suffer loss. The "cost" of love is that it must be present everywhere for anyone to have it and for no reason at all. No one can suffer for the Will of God to be fulfilled for only then can all be recognized as one. On the foundation of these simple statements is sanity restored to perception and another world remembered.

Where Love Would Lead

The desire for Love is the Presence of your God Self expressing its need to join. Miracles happen when we surrender our perception's need for separation and follow this urging. We frequently miss where love would lead us because we feel vulnerable in the places it would take us. We have not yet learned to see a call for love when our ego says we are attacked. Expose the world to miracles. Listen to love's call and follow where it would lead you. This is the practice of forgiveness that will change our mind and allow a loving world to appear.

Love Is Always There

The ego needs to plan in order to control and preserve the status quo. To be "in the moment" opens the mind to trusting an awareness not of the ego. It is an essential step of transferring the power we give to the world of fear and conflict to the unseen Presence of the God Self that is holding the awareness of Truth for us. Your will and the Will of God are forever one. You cannot change yourself because you cannot change the Will of God. Only the *awareness* of your holy perfection can change. The sole function of our learning is to let go of the old ideas that hide our awareness of this Truth. Forgive what you have seen before and allow your mind to see what is really there. Love, and the miracles it brings, is always there to fill the space that hate has left.

Happiness Thoughts

In Mind, which in truth is where we live, thoughts that connect us to one another are what bring us happiness. Being connected is what makes us feel complete. It is the feeling of being loved. Believing we are a separate body in a world where nothing can join, our thoughts of loss bring us the experience of suffering as we sense there is something missing. We are, however, given a way to find what we thought was missing; to remember that we are joined. It is to see our brother's holiness as God created him, before we imagined he could tell a story that could change him and make a world where we would forget that without him part of our Self would be missing. Remember this when you are tempted to condemn the Source of your happiness. When you choose the truth, you Cannot Be Unhappy.

The nature of love is to be inclusive; there is no
awareness of where it cannot be. If you would know
love lives in you, you must also know it lives in
everyone. If you do not recognize it everywhere
you have denied it lives in you.

Guidance

Guidance is not something we need to ask for or even be able to hear for it to function in, and change our lives. God has placed an awareness in our consciousness to do this for us. Jesus tell us: *"No needs will long be left unmet if you leave them all to Him whose function is to meet them. That is His function, and not yours."* Then, in lesson 135, *"What could you not accept if you but knew that everything that happens, all events past, present and to come, are gently planned by one whose purpose is your good?"* There is a "plan" in place that will unfold for us, if we do not over-ride it with one of our own. With God's Plan already laid out for us, our responsibility is not to be tempted to make another one for ourselves.

A Local Call

If you ever feel lonely or depressed, alone and unloved, pick up your mental phone, select the 1 button and talk to God. You will never get a "busy" signal or put on hold. He will talk to you and it is guaranteed to dissolve your worries every time. And, you can do this as often as you like; there is no charge. Heaven is a local call.

Real Choices

Making real choices can change your belief and so can change your world. To make a real choice it is necessary to tell the difference in what you are choosing between. Within the ego's perception there are no real choices to be made. All beliefs there are the same; all are founded on the misperception that sin and separation are real. Choosing between good and bad fundamentally changes nothing because neither choice expresses what is true. All real choices now are between what is real and what is illusion; what arises from perception or exists in the Vision of the God Self. Forgive the perception of both good and bad and there is nothing to challenge your choice for love.

Giving And Receiving Are The Same

There is a time I realize that what I want most is to be loving in every moment, regardless of how that "moment" unfolds in the world. I feel a sureness of this thought for a time and then my mind begins to doubt. I ask why I can't seem to hold the feeling. I hear Brother say, *"How long you are able to hold the feeling of loving your brother is determined by how long you are willing to hold a loving thought of yourself."*

An Exercise In Seeing

Forgiveness is an exercise in seeing. It begins with remembering that what your physical eyes see is not true. The world that appears on the mirror of our mind is not made by God. It is a story of sin and it is not true. But it will continue to appear on the screen of our belief until we refuse to accept the reality of sin. When our thoughts no longer look for sin we will not find it in the world. Seek for holiness instead. Free your mind to find its loving Self. It is a choice, as what you now see is also a choice. And each choice depends on what you want to find. If you are ever to find your loving Self you must make loving choices to remind you of what you are.

Love is both the expression and the experience of
our wholeness. When you love unconditionally,
nothing is lacking in your life.

When I Feel A Sense Of Loss . . .

When I feel a sense of loss at giving up the world my ego thoughts have made, I hear, *"You can only lose what has caused you pain. What God Gives is permanently loving."*

Justice

Justice, in the ego's world, is the measure of the appropriate payment due to atone for a "wrong." It is the means we use to justify revenge and deflect our personal guilt. We believe punishment is needed to deter someone from behaving badly, but just the opposite is true. Bad behavior results from feeling badly about yourself, and punishment is no deterrent because it is what we expect and want as a result of that feeling. No one who feels good about their self acts in a way harmful to others. The next time you are tempted to condemn someone for doing something wrong, ask the God Self what you can do to help them feel better about who they are. Then notice how much better you feel about who you are. Remember, the justice you dispense for others is what you give yourself.

forgiveness by *forgiveness*, our thoughts are changing from you and me to us and we.

The Grace of God

Most of us have forgotten that the Grace of God eternally exists within our Mind. The veil of guilt obscures that now. We do not remember that love, not fear, is the most "natural" of all our feelings; is, in fact, all we would feel if we were free of guilt. Forgiveness expresses an intention of accepting our innocence by withholding judgment. This is enough to open our mind to the Vision of Love the God Self holds for us. Here we find there is no real reason not to love, and discover that being free means simply to disavow that sin is real.

Real Forgiveness

Real forgiveness is not about specific changes to your perception. Real forgiveness recognizes there is no truth in perception; nothing there to really judge between. And in the refusal to judge any aspect of it, perception is recognized as meaningless and can be abandoned entirely. But do this with the knowing that the awareness of your God Self is already there to take its place. Now, with nothing unacceptable, no need to blame anyone for anything, we can accept the truth of our oneness. And we discover that as our perception goes away, only love remains.

The Purpose of The World

The purpose of the world is to lessen our guilt by making others guilty. This inevitably leads to frustration, for no matter how we try to project our guilt it still remains with us. Isolation and loneliness are the only lasting effects of judgment. It has never brought relief from the pain of guilt; never kept us safe from an attack. Sin is not real. It is unknown to God. It exists now in our world only because of a misperceived belief, kept alive through judgment. Forgive yourself and choose to see a world that love has made. Love your brother and discover the Love God has for you.

Seeing Differently

Seeing differently is not about how to see what is painful in a loving way. Seeing differently is about changing the perspective from which you see; shifting from the ego's perception that sin and separation are real, to the Vision of the Holy Spirit that only Love is real. In this awareness there is no belief in sin, no thoughts of pain and suffering in the mind that sees the world and so none to be found in the world it sees. The world we see mirrors only our thoughts about it. When you have accepted there is only love in the reality of the Mind you share with God, Heaven is all you will see.

Joining In The World

We cannot expect to know what joining is within the story of the world. There is no joining when we measure ourselves by such things as intelligence or skill, charisma or the desire to financially succeed, or any other standard whose purpose is to point out differences. The purpose of everything within the world that separation has made must make separation seem real. But it was the desire for "someone else" to share our guilt that gave rise to the need for separation. Accept the unreality of sin and guilt and separateness and there will be no reason not to love your brother unconditionally.

Change What You *Want* To See

The reason the escape from pain and suffering seems so elusive is that we are continuously trying to correct what is wrong with us when there is nothing wrong with us. We merely misperceive what is real and true. It is an error in our thinking that we can correct. The Vision our God Self holds of what is real and true does not tell us we *can be* free. It sees us free now! Correct what you see by changing what you want to see. Make forgiveness the evidence of your intention to see the innocence of God's Creation, in spite of what the world insists is real. Let forgiveness teach you there is peace and love where pain and suffering now seems to be. Awaken the power of your will to see what is real by forgiving what you have judged and surrendering to your desire to love.

Loving Cannot Be Rationalized

If you find yourself thinking about "why" you love someone, pause and realize you are vastly limiting, as well as distorting, your true feelings for them. "Reasons" to love means there are also reasons not to love. To fully appreciate the power of your loving is to recognize there is nothing that can, in truth, oppose it. Thinking there is, is what gives rise to all illusions. The thought of sin and separation could not exist in our awareness if it were absorbed with your true loving nature. If we are ever to be free of our story of sin we must be willing to love "unreasonably," for it is this kind of love that defines what we are.

God's Gift Of Life

Without the fear of death the Love of God is instantly remembered. It is the belief in death that is the egos "proof" our guilt is real and death the answer to "God's demand" for atonement. Believing this, we can see where the ego's fear of God comes from and why it feels a need to maintain a sense of separateness from Him. In truth, it is only our guilt we fear, but each judgment we make of one another to satisfy that guilt becomes another layer of fear separating us from deserving to be loved ourselves. Lets agree to forgive our guilt, let go the need to die and join in our willingness to accept the Love God offers. Lets accept Gods gift of life for everyone who now thinks that they must die.

Do You Want To Know The Truth?

Even a Child of God cannot decide what is true because Who and What He is, is a truth he cannot accept. But having denied our identity there is one thing we must decide; do we want to know the truth? Believing we are "sinful," we have made a perception to take the place of truth, thinking that the truth would condemn us. Now we must decide what we want. We literally make that choice with each decision whether to judge or to forgive. It cannot be too strongly stated, every judgment makes sin real and keeps us prisoner to its despair. And every forgiving thought turns an enemy into a friend and in the joining allows love to remember what is true.

f

Fixing

Healing is not seeing someone fixed that I perceive to be sick. Healing is holding the Holy Spirit's Vision that, in truth, they remain as perfect as God created them. Healing is not about fixing our story. It is about letting the story go.

The belief in sin denies the reality of love. Real forgiveness denies the reality of sin. Real forgiveness demonstrates love has no opposite.

Love Is Everywhere

Love is everywhere we choose to see it for Love created everything that lives and created it like Itself. When we do not see love it is because we have chosen to ignore what Love created and tried to make of it something of our egos choosing. When hate or suffering is what we see we have tried to replace Loves Presence with our story of sin. It is important that we remember love does not come and go. Love is everywhere we bring it, for love is what we are

Heaven Is A Forever Place

Love loses its meaning, its very purpose, in separateness. Love is Creation extending Itself with the unshakable assurance it will forever be the same. Here is our truth that peace and joy are never lost; that Heaven is a forever Place. We do not lose Loves Presence in our Mind in our stories of being separate, but we do deprive ourselves of the incredible peace and joy our acceptance of it brings. Consider for a moment that there is no one you would not love in the innocence of their creation. Now forgive your story of separateness and time and let that moment live again.

Letting Change Be Made For Us

When I am perceiving myself as separate and individual and attempt to change "my" mind, only my story of being separate and different is affected. When I recognize that my story is only a different version of all stories, then ask our God Self to use my intention to change our consciousness, that change will affect all of consciousness because His Vision of me is as a part of the whole. Using my perception to change the way I see does nothing to free anyone from the idea that separation is real. But all change implemented by the God Self affects the whole consciousness because that is His intention for it. Our function is to bring the egos intention to Him, desiring the change but trusting Him to make it for us all.

Love is elusive when finding guilt is important.

Never underestimate the power of a loving choice.
It has the ability to induce miracles of every nature,
everywhere in our consciousness. Heaven is
remembered in unconditionally loving relationships.
And in them is misperception healed, for the myth
of separation does not exist in loves presence.

A Christmas message from our Brother:

"Let this time become a celebration of Who and What we are. Let us express our gratitude by sharing God's Gift to us with all those who are troubled and in pain. Let us hold the awareness of the Holy Spirits Presence in them that they may know their innocence and feel again God's Love for them. Know as you give this gift it is the one thing that will heal all ills, bring peace to our troubled mind and restore the awareness of our one Self. Add your certainty to mine that it may become a light for all to see and follow. Then join with me in giving thanks to our Father for having given us this gift to give."

The path to awakening seems long because of the distance we keep between us.

Our Relationship With God

All relationships have the potential to reflect your relationship with God. The Light of God's Love is "born" in everyone at the instant of their creation. As deeply as it may be hidden under the layers of our self-denial, it is immediately available to us in the Vision our God Self holds. It is this Light, this Love, that is the basis for all our seeking, and it is revealed to us as we forgive the stories in which It has been lost. Ask simply to see the spark of God's Love that has blossomed into your brother and you will recognize what makes you One with him.

172

This World Is Not My Home

When I feel a loss and look outward at the world expecting to find there what will console and make me feel whole again, nothing changes; the sense of loss persists. Then I hear my inner Voice call to me and I turn within. I by-pass all the ego strongholds where bodies and the stories they tell seem real. I reach another "world" untouched by sadness and time. Here there is nothing missing, nothing I need to gain. And everyone is here; both those that seemed to have moved on and those still pretending to tell an "earthly" story. Here there is only peace and joy and love beyond measure. I will rest here for a while. I may return then to my other world, but I now know that it is not my home.

Joining

When any two consciously choose to engage with the God Self together, the effects far exceed what could occur if each had done so alone. Feeling the wholeness, the completeness of all things comes with the simple intention to join with what is part of you, though long denied. And joining in the Presence of the God Self also brings the Vision, the awareness of Love's Presence to you. In that instant when you are free of the idea of sin and the need to be different you see the magnitude of what Love really is. In but a moment you are aware there has been nothing but a thought, an untrue thought, that seemed to separate you from Paradise Itself. This is the "reward" of forgiveness, finding what was hidden but never lost.

A New Years Resolution

As one year passes and another takes its place, I let my thoughts of sin and separateness, of fear and judgment, pass along with them. I choose now to accept instead my holiness, along with yours, and welcome a forgiven world into our mind. I choose to believe that uninterrupted peace and joy await us in this world and that every thought here begins with a love that draws us together. I trust that should I falter in my resolve, there is a light in us that you will hold for me until I have remembered. I know I do not make this choice alone, for that could never be. We go to truth together or we go there not at all. So take my hand as I take another. Together we will form a network of love that will embrace and heal the whole world.

Wanting vs. Deserving

We are Beings of spirit / mind. Our experience is determined by our thoughts and the meaning we give them. When we do not question what we deserve, we are free to have what we want. This is particularly true as it concerns our desire to be loved. Forgive your brother his every undeserving thought and discover how loved you really are.

The Cost Of Hating

As long as you think it is possible to hate someone you are lost to the experience of being wholly loved. Seeking love from a source you perceive to be "outside" yourself is your admission it does not exist within you. And where love is not perceived there will be a form of hate, for it is only hate, or by its other name of fear, that the mind denies its natural inclination to love. It is as we remove each block to love and find love there to instantly take its place that we come to learn what is "natural" about us. But Love does have one condition that governs recognition of what it really is: It has no opposite. You are eternal because Love is what you are.

Where Nothing Opposes Love

There is a "world" where nothing opposes love. It isn't now beyond our grasp, some far away place. We can go there in an instant, the very moment we forgive someone we thought we could not love; the moment it dawns upon us we cannot change the Will of the One Who only loves. In this moment is our own desire to love released from sin's restrictions and freed to recognize Itself. In that moment is the world that love has made, but kept hidden by our "brother's" guilt, now free to be accepted and therefore seen. Love now is recognized as all we want, for it alone expresses what we are.

When Fear Arises

When fear arises it is because we have forgotten Who walks with us. Fear is the sense of being alone, which, in turn, only seems possible when we feel unloved or unloving. Learning to ask for guidance throughout the day, for even the most mundane choices, keeps us aware of the constant Presence of our holy and wholly loving Self; the Presence of all Creation. When the dark moments then seem to come we have the means to quickly surrender those thoughts because we have established the reality of the Presence being there to help us, to remind us that we are indeed wholly loved and never alone.

The Holy Ego

It is good to renew our desire to have a helpful and loving purpose in the world. If it relies on the ego's need to correct an injustice or fix the world in some way, we have again entrusted our healing to the source that sees a need to have pain. It is easy to know when this happens for the ego's goals are conflicted, with no intention of ever being reached. Our purpose here is to be witness to God's Love; to clear from our mind the myth of sin and of fear. This is not something our "holy" ego can do. So when things are not going smoothly, it is time for a "reality" check. Go to your place of Refuge. Rest there with Him Who loves you. Then give Him your willingness to love, and your purpose has now been fulfilled.

forgiving is the gift of love, for giving love unites the giver and who receives the gift as one.

What Is Broken?

When I am sick or experiencing any of fears effects, the experience seems real and so the thought of healing comes from the belief that something is broken and needs to be fixed. Here I must remember that it is necessary for the God Self to be the One in charge of healing because He is not confused by the seeming reality of sickness or fear. He does not try to fix what is broken which would only make the illusion real and change nothing. He corrects the illusion by seeing that nothing real happened; our real Self was never threatened. Changing our perception will change the form of our illusion, but it is the God Self Vision of the truth of our perfect wholeness that dissolves that perception and heals what we see. Every reason not to love others disappears with self-forgiveness. The urge to judge anything is gone when you have accepted yourself. All the symbols of separateness depend upon a single thought: *There must be something wrong with me.* Forgive this thought. Ask to see the whole and complete "you" the God Self sees, not the one that needs to be healed. Now is the Vision of a forgiven world free to rise. Now we are free to love everyone.

Guilt – The Hidden Cause of Our Perception

For many lifetimes, in all cultures, we have struggled to find a sense of self-worth in this world. Our drive to improve ourselves, to measure our worth by what we accomplish is testament to the belief that we are born incomplete.

The cause of this feeling that there is something missing, of the need to prove our self worth, is a guilt so deeply hidden, so "natural," it goes unquestioned. It seems far more fitting to profess our ignorance and inabilities than our talents and loving instincts. When we look out at this world and see all the suffering we cause ourselves and one another, we long for a better way, but not knowing its true cause we don't know how to change it. We have misperceived that the causes of the world are in the world, but it is our thoughts driven by our hidden guilt that are responsible for the heartache and the hatred, the disease and "natural" disasters that happen in our world.

What we will learn as we come to accept that it is we who have made our world is that there is a very simple principle we can apply toward changing our thoughts that have made it: Let our "natural" desire to love replace our "un-natural" need to judge. Without our feelings of guilt, there is nothing to judge and our desire to love, even ourselves, is made free.

Why is our guilt so pervasive? It begins with our belief that we are born in sin—that there is something innately wrong with us. We have made our world as the experience of this belief. We are told it was when "a tiny mad idea" entered the mind of God's Son that he momentarily lost the awareness of his true Self in the dream about this idea. We don't remember this, of course, and any speculation about it serves mostly to make real what has no substance outside the dream. What is important is to realize the idea was insane. We have not changed, cannot change, the nature of the Thought that created us what we are, whole and complete and part of God.

Is it possible to consistently be the Presence of Love in all situations? Free of guilt it is impossible to be anything else.

The Fast Track To Forgiveness

When you discover a brother who appears to be unloving, whose behavior provokes some fear or calls for a "slight" judgment, be grateful. Be grateful you have learned there is a different way to see him; that you have found the Means to see his loving presence. Be grateful you no longer need be burdened with the fears and anger of judging him - or yourself. Learning to make gratitude your first thought is the "fast track" to forgiveness.

The Joy Of God's Reality

A message received by Linda: "*Beloved, your Father has given you the creation of Himself as Love's Perfection. We understand this is not what you now believe about yourself. But, you have a great amount of support to accept this challenge for yourself even now. Remember, this is not a change you are making, you are merely accepting what has been eternally yours. Know as well, that the more you do let go of your resistance, the more support you will become aware of. At this point in your minds focus you perceive this shift as kind of loss, but this is only choices you seem to have, you would not hesitate to choose the joy of God's Reality.*"

Projection Makes Separation

It is mind believing it is guilty, then projecting its guilt, that makes it feel separate from "other" minds. It is to have an "object" to punish for its guilt that mind creates the image of a body as its "self." It is only to fulfill this purpose that the body suffers pain and dies. Forgiveness is God's Plan to end this cycle of lies. As we forgive our brother, his guilt and ours goes away. With guilt gone, the purpose of the body can be changed. Suffering and death are not needed. Be determined to see everyone sinless. In the absence of guilt love will arise and we will see a different world. Together we can do this!

How Far Is Heaven?

How far away is Heaven? Take someone's hand and together proclaim, *"There is no guilt in us for there is none in God. We will accept no thought that would make us different from each other or from our one Source."* Then together reach out your hand and take God's Hand that welcomes you home. In this moment you realize that only Love is real and recognize you are in Heaven now, for there is no other place to be.

Attack the Son, Attack The Father

When you think we are all separate you cannot see that to attack any brother, regardless of the reason, is an attack upon the Father Who created his Son exactly like Himself. But, in truth, God's Mind cannot be turned against Itself and so all thoughts of attack are self attack and are meaningless. What has no effect cannot be real. Do we need another "reason" to forgive?

Our ego would like to experience a better world, if only "they" would change. The God Self suggests a perfect world already exists when I am ready to see the perfection in my brother.

The God Self

Who we are is what the God Self Is. We don't stop being this when we lose our focus and behave like an ego. What we lose is our awareness of who we are. But we should keep in mind God's Awareness of us hasn't changed. His Plan for us continues to unfold perfectly. We only get in the way when we think we have failed our "shoulds." We are changing our thinking which is the cause of our habits of doing. We have not left our Father's Mind. We have not stopped being His Own Thought. This is the Vision the God Self holds. In accepting this from Him we welcome Him into our awareness and in this way He changes our mind for us.

Loving Yourself

The willingness to love yourself can seem to be the most difficult task you will ever undertake. Left to the ego's perception it will seem impossible because perception is founded on the belief there is something wrong with us. We have perfected the art of projecting our "sins" onto our brothers, but beneath them all remains the conviction we are unlovable. Yet the willingness to see and love *all of* God's Creation is fundamental to awakening to the truth. Loving is the movement of Creation and we are the means thru which it moves. Loving yourself removes the feeling that something is wrong with you and relieves you of the need to project unloving feelings onto others. Now the door is open to extending love and remembering our one true function. Let the God Self show you how to love yourself and so open your heart to everyone.

Choosing Between Illusions

Every choice made between illusions strengthens the belief in all illusions. To refuse to judge one illusion calls all judgment into question. Practice forgiveness, even when you think there is nothing real to forgive. Practice bringing illusions to the truth, darkness to the light and fear to love, and watch truth and light and love prevail. The intention to let truth in must ultimately succeed because truth is already here.

When you finally find your Self you will realize you have never been lost.

The Compelling Belief In Differences

When you see hatred or suffering in the world it is, in the egos reasoning, easy to conclude that we are a long way from having world peace. This seems obvious because we see these "perpetrators" as different, with little recognition of the truth, while we who are more "advanced," are relatively more peaceful. We do not recognize that the differences we see in "them" exist only to validate our belief that we are all different and separate. If the idea of differences was not needed to support the misperception of sin, we would recognize that "they" are a part of us, their story of death and destruction another version of political strife or financial hardship. We are parts of a single, whole consciousness, whether we think of it as an ego consciousness, or the Creation of God. Let forgiveness dissolve your need to be different and expect the world to be more peaceful. We move as one, or not at all.

Everyone shares the desire to be loved, but that desire goes unfulfilled until we recognize it is a part of our need to give love. What a simple formula – give more to get more of what you want!

*f*orgiveness will be an intellectual
concept when used to overlook the egos behavior.
It becomes a profound tool for healing when you
hear your Voice for Truth whisper: "It didn't
happen!"

Each time you are tempted to judge someone for
anything, say, "I am sinless," and watch the need to
judge go away.

The Illusion Of A Self

We have created an illusion of our Self, an image of a being
separated from its real Creator. We call this illusion of our
real Self an ego. We use our Mind to judge this ego and all
the "other" egos that appear and so make a war between
them; a war against our Self. Now we are lost in the battles
they perform, needing to judge which is right and which is
wrong. Yet what is there to win in a battle of illusions? We are
so lost we do not see that it is God we battle with; trying to
replace His beloved Son with this character we have made.
Step back a moment from this war into the Presence of your
God Self. There is an ancient memory held for us there of
eternal loving and being loved. Affirm that this is where you
want to be and let the madness of the illusion be replaced by
the Peace of God.

"Not One More Holy Than The Rest"

I once asked Brother how he so easily overlooked the pain he suffered from those who had so harshly condemned him to crucifixion. Before he answered I found myself witnessing the scene again. Anger and accusations seemed to come from everywhere. But it was the sense of fear coming from those judging him I noticed most. Then he said, *"Now see it through my eyes."* I began to feel his loving presence, a feeling I had come to know by then. The heaviness, the fear, the sense of conflict lifted and soon was gone. The room, in fact, was replaced by a feeling of pure light. He said, *"All those present in judgments chamber that day were God's Sons, not one more holy than the rest."* I try to remember this when I am tempted to find value in any judgment I might make.

Fear And Guilt

Fear can only control you if you believe you are guilty of something. Salvation comes with the belief you cannot change what God created sinless. Our stories of horror are of the ego's making (bodies hurting bodies) and have not touched or changed the spirit being God created. It is a question of what we will believe is real and true: What God created or what we have made. Is the world real? Ego thoughts may arise but will only be fearful if you believe you have created yourself.

Perfect Oneness

ACIM is, after all, a course in mind training. I sometimes forget, the training is to learn how to accept Oneness, not separateness as what is real and true; to learn that Heaven is our real goal, not to make a better world. It is to remember that Heaven is *"not a place nor a condition. It is merely an awareness of perfect Oneness, and the knowledge that there is nothing else; nothing outside this Oneness, and nothing else within."* Heaven is here. Heaven is now. Heaven is all there is without the thought of separation. Let us join here and now and allow that thought to become our reality.

To Know God

To know God, recognize He is your brother's creator; that all Creation is an extension of all that your brother Is. Each time, then, that you call your brother's name and bring his presence into your awareness, God's Presence must be there too. Now when you are tempted to judge an image the ego would make of your brother, remember that God is also there. See past the image perception has made to what is really there. To know God is to know where to find Him. And then you must find Him in everything you see.

The real purpose of a loving relationship is not to learn to love each other, but simply to learn to love.

187

Listen . . . Do you hear God calling, asking for your help? It may sound like a brother asking to be loved. Or a sister wanting to be reassured. We have many opportunities to hear Him call, if we will be still a moment and just listen. Make this the purpose of your world, to hear Him call and offer you the gift to see and bless His holy Child that He created one with you. To love each one without a thought of what his dream is that we condemned before. Bless each one until you have blessed them all and the whole world is brightened by the love you have given.

forgiving

If you look at the world and see all the pain and suffering, the hatred and attack that seems to be there, you will likely come to the conclusion that forgiveness of the whole world is too much a stretch for you. Remind yourself then that everything you see "out there" is a mirror for how you see yourself. To forgive is to see without sin. Not to be able to forgive reflects something "unforgivable" we see within ourselves. To truly forgive and be able to love again is to recognize that sin cannot be real because it is not present in the Thought of God; does not exist in His Love for His Creation. All forgiveness then, begins with forgiving yourself for having condemned what God has created in perfect Love.

A Call For Love

When fear arises, rather than push it away, try to recognize it is a call for love from the part of you that does not believe it can be loved. It is helpful here to separate the dreamer from his dream. Open your heart to your God Self and feel God's Love embrace you. Accept the reality of the dreamer by denying the reality of his dream. Your brother is here to help you remember who you are, as you are here to help him. Forgive his dreams for him and let him love you so both can better remember your purpose here. This is the universal call for love we must learn to respond to in order to allow our dreams of fear to be changed to happy dreams.

Love Is Not An Option

Loves Presence is not an option. It is a certainty. The option is whether we will recognize and accept that it is always with you. Find one you have judged responsible for love not being present in the world. Forgive him. See his reality. Stay with the feeling until you are free of your accusation. Now embrace him with all the love you would normally reserve for God and discover Loves presence in the world. As this miracle unfolds you will witness your story that the world is real fade into the dream it really is. Do this if you would like to know how it is possible to love yourSelf.

The Source Of Healing

Letting go of the need to be separate is the source of all healing. When you choose to see your innocence choose also to see your brother's innocence as well. Your innocence without his is meaningless. Because he is a part of you, your choice for yourself alone is incomplete. Yet it must then be also true that when you choose for him your intention strengthens and makes clear for everyone that our real goal is Oneness. Let the acceptance of your brother's holiness, joined with yours, be the witness of a forgiven world.

Love Has No Opposite

Sin cannot be real for there is no opposite to love. It is the illusion that we have lost our "connection" to Love that has given rise to all illusions. Forgive what cannot be true. Refuse to judge illusions and allow the God Self to lift this burden from our mind. You cannot control or change the ego's consciousness while seeing yourself as a separate individual. This is the function of the God Self Who knows that "all" are one. Teach yourself that you can rely on our God Self by trusting Him to perform the function God gave Him to do.

The Divine Plan

The "divine Plan" for our awakening is already in place. On the highest level of our awareness it has already happened. The implementation of the Plan is functioning perfectly simply because it is God's Will that we remember His Love and our Oneness with Him. Our recognition that the Plan is working is a function of whether we put our trust in His Plan, or try to "improve" upon it with our own plan. Forgive every thought that prevents you from loving yourself and joining with your brother and watch God's Plan more easily unfold.

Are you ready to release yourself from sin? If so, you must not judge anything you see in the world as real, for everything there has been made to validate the reality of sin.

God Is Present

Jesus frequently reminds us that the memory of God is forever in our mind. I ask how to best awaken that memory. He replies, *"In the willingness to love yourself."* And how do I do that, I ask. *"Ask to see your brother before you cast the shadow of sin upon him. When Love no longer is denied its Source will be remembered."* The Light has come. God is present, here and now.

There is no one in whom the Light of God's Love is not present. Whether or not I see it is the measure of how attached I am to the belief there is something wrong with me.

The purpose of all relationships is to find the loving Self we have disguised as a guilty brother.

The belief that I feel a need to change myself is testament to who I believe created me.

Your Call For Love

It is good to be reminded that when the world's suffering and seeming lack of love tend to overwhelm us, these experiences arise because they best reflect what we think is true. It is easy to forget when we blame a brother for his shortcomings we bring lack into our own lives. Or when we accuse him of attacking us it is the same thought we use to condemn ourselves, bringing guilt and sickness to our experience. We do not recognize that accepting sin and separation as real brings all the accompanying thoughts that support it. So when angry or fearful or unloving thoughts about others appear, remind yourself who suffers their consequences. Then forgive yourself for attacking yourself and feel your God Self answering your call for love.

Merging Minds

What you see thru the perception of separateness will appear to be different and functioning apart from you and everything else. But in truth nothing can exist apart from you, and so you have the power to change the meaning and the purpose of everything in your awareness. Picture yourself connected to everything you can think of, its form and its function now being irrelevant. The world that once seemed "out there," now fits nicely into this picture. Hold this thought and feel the dimension of your mind expand to embrace a truth it had forgotten, but now begins to remember. Now thoughts of your brother flow freely into your picture and you welcome the feeling of connection that has drawn them there. Your "seeing" and theirs begins now to merge as you feel the love of your joining. Here your awareness of what is real will change. For here you now feel what it means to be whole.

When you wonder why it sometimes seems that fear is stronger than love, recall how often you practice using each of them. We will always rely upon what we believe serves us best. The more you practice relying on love the stronger it will become in your experience.

Perception and Truth

If you think your perception is the truth and then experience the thoughts that arise from it fearfully, you have associated fear with truth and you will be afraid to find the truth of yourself. It is this thinking that has led us to fear the Will of God, firmly establishing the "reality" of fear and the weakness of love. If you want to be free of fear let this awareness be your motivation for turning more to the God Self for guidance. Learn to associate fear with illusion, truth with love and you will come to know your will and the Will of God are one.

The Power Of Love

Few have yet realized the value and the power of the Love residing in them. This recognition does not come until we have let go the seeking of things that have no real value. Its meaning will remain elusive until loving a brother and loving yourself merge into one desire. But come it must for love alone defines the nature of your Being. There will be a moment when you look into a brothers eyes and see reflected there all you have ever searched for. You will see a Light so radiant and pure the thought of sin will lose its meaning; a feeling of joy that only God's Love could express. And you will recognize it is your Self you have found in him. This holy encounter awakens the truth in both of you and throughout the one consciousness. You will know then you are free to come Home, for you have found your Fathers lost Son.

The Benefit Of Giving

When you feel called upon to give love to someone your ego tells you is undeserving, you feel a sense of sacrifice, as though you are "losing" something by giving it. Just the opposite, however, is true. It was only your feeling deprived of love that made you reluctant to give it. But in the act of giving you now discover what you didn't know you had. A brother never asks of you what you would not benefit from by giving it. It is not possible for one to lose while another gains. Giving and receiving are the same. It is all an exchange within our one Self, a mutual satisfying of every need or desire we perceive to have. Recognize this and you have taken a giant stride toward accepting the reality of our Oneness.

f

Free Will

Free will is not the latitude to make true what is not true. It is not possible to separate your will from the Will that created you and so make a different "truth" to govern your experience. And if you are confused about whether it is love or fear that God made real before the world began, ask yourself which would have been your will if the choice were yours. Ultimately it will be your choice to decide which you will accept as true. Seeing it in this way makes it clear that free will is always about what you really want to be true.

A Witness To Your Innocence

The ego will not learn to heal itself. Its thought of sickness exists to prove that sin and separation is real. Healing is brought to us with the awareness that God's Son cannot be sick because God cannot be sick and His Son cannot be different or apart from What created him, whole and as a part of Its One Self. Accept the God Self as a witness to your innocence then become your brother's witness to what is true for everyone.

f

The Moment Of Truth

Every moment of every day is a moment when truth is available to replace our illusions. For truth is in full bloom within our mind, this very instant. It will only seem to grow as we accept this single thought: Sin is not real. Forgive this one thought now and be willing to see a happy world arise to replace the one we have made a prisoner of fear. Remove the thought of sin from your mind and let the world become a haven of peace and safety. There is no world but this one within our mind. There is no darkness there but disguises the Light of His perfect Love. Choose this moment to be the one you will accept God's Gift of Truth and free the world to be a mirror for His Love.

Don't ever feel you have to pursue your awakening or face your challenges alone. If you can't find the Presence of your God Self, call upon a friend for help. God is present everywhere so any friend will do.

You are not the character in the story you are telling. You are dreaming of a "self" you think you "ought" to be. Stop dreaming. See your brother innocent and only the truth of the storyteller will remain.

God Needs Your Love

Loving support and guidance are always with us. They are a natural function of a joined mind in harmony with Itself, expressing love as its only purpose. It is our awareness of this that comes and goes, depending mostly on whether we feel deserving to be loved. When you feel disconnected and unable to hear, ask the God Self to bring you someone who needs your love. Watch as you give love how it comes back to you. Notice as you connect in love, that there is also no one else you cannot welcome there. Now notice that what you could not "hear" before has come into your mind. Whatever the question seemed to be, loving is always the answer.

When your identity is in doubt, check the label imprinted on your soul: **MADE IN HEAVEN.**

The Vision Of Love

Awakening is about learning to recognize Love where it now is and always has been. ACIM tells us it is a course in learning how to "see differently," to tell the difference between truth and illusion. That doesn't mean being able to look on pain and suffering and see it differently. It means finding the Presence of Love within you that does not see the story of pain and suffering because, in truth, it does not exist in God's Creation. Do not be tempted to reconcile truth with illusion. They are irreconcilable. To forgive sin is to recognize it cannot co-exist with love and therefore cannot exist at all. Ask to see only what love sees and allow a world of holiness to take the place of a world of fear. This is the miracle of real forgiveness. This is how you exercise your role as a Creator and extender of Truth.

When you don't feel good about yourself it must be because you have accepted the ego's evaluation. Don't be frustrated because you expect it to be accepting; and don't try to teach it how to love. That is not the role the ego plays. Ask instead to be shown the Face of Christ. There is no confusion there that you are loved.

Your Connection To Love

Past all of mind's meanderings in time and space, just before the thought of sin, nothing existed in all creation that did not love you and nothing existed you did not love. There seems now to be a world of sin to separate us from what we love yet this world rests entirely on our wish that it be there. We have imagined the thought of sin and affirm that it is what we want with every judgment we choose to make. There is another world that remembers love and will arise when we again want love more than we want guilt. Please remember when next you are tempted to condemn, you make a choice to value sin and relinquish your connection to love.

Forgiveness is to help us stop seeing what is not really there.

Love Is All I Have

Every attack begins within my mind. Its target is always my guilty self, even when I try to "share" my guilt with others by judging them for my "sins." Yet what is attacked is just a story; a character I pretend is me. Every desire to love is also born within my mind. Its purpose is to see and extend a loving self. Both "selves" seem to be there, even when I think it is only the loving one I want. But my mind will seem to be split between loving and not loving until I have forgiven my guilt and know that I am lovable. Only then will I recognize it is only love that possesses; that it is all I have to give.

199

The Voice For God

I have asked our Brother to give us a message to begin the year. This is what he has said and I want to share it with you.

 A New Years Resolution

This is the time when you review your life and decide if you will make different choices for your future. Pause for a moment and reflect on whether this process has ever fulfilled the expectations you have had for it. I ask you to consider there is but a single choice you must make if you would bring happiness and peace to your life experience. Indeed, just this one choice can you make if peace and happiness is what you truly want.

Resolve to be the Voice for God. All other choices expect too little and so must leave you unfulfilled. Resolve that it will be His Eyes you use to see, His Heart to decide the worth of everything. His ears will determine what you hear; His Voice will speak the words that all will know to be the truth.

Resolve that by your presence everyone will know that they are loved. Let no one escape the healing joy of your forgiveness! Let nothing of his story distract you from your goal. It is time now for sin and guilt, lack and suffering and every other denial of your wholeness to be put aside. There is no reason for you not to love! I ask this of you because to ask less would be meaningless to the Holy Child of God.

Resolve that your strength of trust will be the bridge across which all may walk to find a loving world. As you accept your role and allow God's Plan to effortlessly unfold through you, you have become the world's witness that love through forgiveness answers every need.

If, as you consider these things that I suggest you are tempted to doubt your resolve, then in that moment use my strength of trust in you. Let me be the bridge to your place of trust, as I ask you to do for others. Accept my assurance as though it were your own, for such is the bond we share. There is no point where I begin and where you end. Only in the ego's world can distinction be made between us.

Do not dwell on how difficult this may seem or how long you can hold to your resolve. Join me but for a moment and let that be enough. Then join me for another moment when you can, and another after that. See each one complete unto itself and you will have no fear of loss.

Resolve to be the Voice for God for that is what you are. Decide that you can give the world all that this implies for only in the giving of it will you recognize that it is yours. Only as you are witness that everyone is loved can you accept God's promise of what you are. Join with me now that together we are the vision that answers and heals the world's need for separateness. Join with me that together all of consciousness may now find and share the peace and strength that is in our Oneness, and remember at last what it means to Love.

What Does Our Brother Want?

What does our brother or our sister really want of us? It's easy to be deceived. But no matter how it looks, you will find it is exactly what you want of them. We have tried to project our self-guilt onto them to make them "worse" than we. And they have done the same. But when we realize we both are looking to be loved we can find love within ourselves to give and join with him.

Being Content With Who We Are

Some have concern they would lose all sense of identity were they to surrender into and become a part of the one, whole Self. Just the opposite is true. When forgiveness has let thoughts of sin fall away, removing the need to be separate, only love remains. Here there is nothing to be lost as the whole Self merges into you and you recognize you have always been one with It. Then we can finally see it was only the images made from guilt and suffering we had been reluctant to let go. Now we are content with Who we *are without our story.*

Accepting Yourself

Accept yourself unconditionally and you will love everyone you see and recognize they are part of you. How do you accept yourself unconditionally? For an instant, see yourself without a past, without your story of the world.

Recognizing The Holy Instant You Have Asked For

Today, when the first inclination to judge a brother arises in your mind, ask your God Self to show you that God, Presence of all that is loving, is present right now in the one you are about to judge. Recognizing your brother past the ego's perception is the holy instant you have been waiting for. Treasure this recognition. Ask to be reminded of this moment whenever you are tempted to judge. This is the miracle of real forgiveness.

Neither rush to nor resist the thought of letting the body go. Focus instead on your willingness to accept everything that lives as a part of you.

The body is not the evidence of life. The evidence of life is the desire to love.

Love Sees Only Love

Are you willing to see love everywhere? If you want to find it you must see it everywhere for it cannot be divided. Sometimes it seems to masquerade as hate or fear, but if you see love from where it resides in you, you cannot be deceived. Seen correctly then, love sees only love for that is all there is.

Who Are You Without A Body?

Think of your self without a body. It really has nothing to do with who you are and it will one day drop away. Who will you be without it? Think of those you love without a body. If you are free to simply be a "mind," who could you not be with at any time? If you cannot eagerly welcome this thought you have encountered your primary obstacle to the peace and joy inherent in joining. Now would be a good opportunity to let that go.

You cannot remember the sensation of limitless loving while believing your mind is limited to the experience of a body.

A "Universe" of Mind?

What if this vast thing we call a universe that encompasses all that seems to exist in our awareness, was actually a metaphor for your mind? Everything that exists there would be symbols of your thoughts, unfolding in the way that best illustrates the accumulation and blending of those thoughts - your belief. Everyone, then, who shares this world with you, seeing what you see, though frequently giving it a different meaning, also must be sharing this same mind. Then, I wonder, what would I be if I simply acknowledged this world, this mind, all was a part of me?

Be Happy With Who You Are

To love ourselves we must be happy with who we think we are. It means we have finally come to accept ourselves as God created us, like Himself and to reflect His Happiness. We will then be happy with what we see in others, seeing them free of sin and as an extension of our happiness. We will not see the character in their dream for we no longer identify with our own character. The story of sorrow and pain will be gone for they cannot exist in a happy dream. And being happy with them we will join with them, for happiness embraces all it sees. And joined in this embrace of happiness we will recognize our Self and what it means to love. And thus we will fulfill God's Purpose to extend His Happiness and Love to all creation.

Changing Nightmares To Happy Dreams

Changing nightmares to happy dreams is the surest way to let them go. Our relationships, in all their forms, seem to be the cause of our unhappy dreams for they directly reflect the way we judge ourselves. So it is through our relationships the Holy Spirit's Plan will lead us to find a world where our desire to be joined in peace mirrors God's Will for us. All relationships potentially serve this purpose, so if it is a loving, peaceful world you want, ask to be aware of how to use each relationship you have to bring it to you. It will be in doing this we recognize our will and the Will of God are one.

Perception Or Vision?

When what you perceive about yourself is an illusion but you accept it as the truth, it is impossible to distinguish between the truth and illusion of anything. When what you see of yourself is true it is impossible to believe in illusions of any kind. This essentially defines the difference between the ego's perception and the Vision of the God Self. Understanding this it seems obvious which we would choose. Or does it?

Ending The Need For Holocausts

We frequently feel that if we expose in great detail how terrible things, such as the holocaust, have been, we will surely never allow them to occur again. History proves this is not the case. Holocausts, large and small, occur each time I judge myself, or my brother, as unworthy of being loved. Each time I want the stories we tell of hate and fear to be more real than risking to rely on that loving place we share with God, there is a cutting-off in my mind of one that God created brother to me. What ends the need for holocausts is remembering that I am loved and expressing that by sharing the Presence of Love within me with everyone I meet!

What you practice . .

What you practice by the choices you make is what you teach has value. It is your assertion of what you want. Become conscious that every choice you make impacts and influences everyone, everywhere for there is no one that is not a part of you and does not share your mind. Let the understanding of this become truth for you by consciously wanting for everyone what you would give to those you love most.

Do not attempt to "wake up" – find the truth – until you are willing to accept the possibility that there is nothing wrong with you.

All forms of deception disappear when I recognize that whatever I perceive is "wrong" comes directly from the belief there is something wrong with me.

Free To Love Again

The ego's perception, and the world it spawns, is built upon the belief that there is something wrong with us. Every disagreement, angry thought, "natural" disaster, sickness and death, every reason not to love, arises from this single thought. All our struggles to heal disease, fix the environment, or put an end to war, has its source in this thought. Remove this thought and we are free of all its effects. Forgive yourself when anything seems to threaten your peace and we will heal the world and free ourselves to love again.

Risk Being Free

We have the need to make the world as we would have it be because we think we know what will keep us safe, make us happy and feel loved. We do not realize that in the pursuit of our ego goals we actually perpetuate what we are trying to escape. We think what keeps us safe is making someone else responsible for our guilt. We think what will make us happy is finding someone who will love us in spite of all our faults. Yet with each projection we make, with each one we find who will share our guilt, we have solidified and made more real the misperceptions that are the cause of feeling vulnerable, unhappy and unloved. The truth is, we do not know what makes us feel safe, happy or loved. But until we acknowledge this simple fact and let our God Self choose for us, we will continue to try to remodel this world and resist letting go of all the misperceptions that make it seem real. All of them. For as long as we think we do know, all we perceive to be true remains an illusion. Our trust still remains with what we fear, and what will set us free is what seems to be the dream. Say then to your God Self, "Choose for me. I am ready to risk being free.

If there is one thing you find unforgivable then no real forgiveness is possible because you have left forgiveness to the judgment of the ego's story. Give every reason not to love to the One Who knows you are not in this story and you will free all the world to love again.

The journey to Truth seems long because of the distance we keep between us.

When you ask for healing, or the wisdom to be happy, ask it for everyone. To choose for yourself alone only ensures you will experience being alone.

Say aloud to a group of friends: "I have no guilt, I can do no wrong, cause no pain to anyone. The world I see is only witness to my dream of sin." When you can do this without shame or feelings of arrogance you will know the power of real forgiveness.

If we are finally to find peace and be free of fear, faith in each other is not an option. Forgive the world you see. Learn to travel light. The time it takes to get to Heaven is directly influenced by the amount of baggage you carry.

Each projection we make solidifies our belief that cause and effect are separate. It is a little like drinking poison and expecting someone else will die.

What is Authentic?

If you accept the world as authentic then what you do there defines your worth and who you are. If you judge what you have done as bad you will see yourself as a bad person with the need to atone for what has made you bad. Unfortunately, once you have judged yourself your guilt will remain for in the ego's judgment there is no atonement. Forgiveness denies the reality of guilt and changes the world's purpose by allowing the natural desire to love to replace the need to judge, and in the presence of love you will know what is authentic.

The one condition love has is that it must be eternally present, everywhere. Our ability to know love is our willingness to see it where it is.

Giving Is Receiving

The cost of giving is receiving. You cannot give what you have not made yours. You will suffer the effects of your self-judgment, or reap the joy of your forgiveness. You will find your innocence each time you refuse to judge someone else. Your experience is the perfect mirror of what you want for your brother. Refusing to judge what is not real frees you from attack. Teach only love and discover that is what you are.

Accepting What We Are

While pursuing our awakening to the truth, it is important to remember that everything we are looking for we already have. All we have a need to learn is already known. The loving being you want to become is who you already are – right now. It is not a matter of becoming something. It is a process of remembering what we have given away. This is important to remember so that we do not use forgiveness to overcome what we fear, but to teach us instead that fear is not real.

You may ignore, even deny the Presence of your God Self. You may not be apart from it, however, for It is who you are.

Two Worlds

It is not complicated. We reinforce our faith in what we believe will sustain us by the choices we make. There are two worlds available to us. We choose to have a loving world with each forgiving thought. We choose a fearful outcome with each judgment that we make. If you don't believe that this is true, keep a journal of the choices that you make. Record the outcome of what your intentions have brought you. Don't deny yourself the joy of loving choices.

Hidden behind the need to feel separate is the knowing there is no one who does not love you and no one you do not love.

Sacrifice Is An Attack On Love

There is a world of difference in love as we now see it and what it really is. To the ego the foundation of love is based on sacrifice. In truth love is the "glue" that binds us together; God's intention for all He created. Sacrifice is an attack on love for it demands that guilt and fear drive apart what God created whole. Forgiveness denies there are conditions to loving and by doing so denies the reality of both guilt and fear. Ask the God Self to forgive your fearful thoughts for you and open your mind to the awareness of the whole and perfect Love of God waiting for you where It has always been.

Love Waiting To Be Recognized

It is our practice of applying the awareness we are learning in the choices we make that changes our "understanding" into our belief. I was at the shopping center when a disheveled person approached my car and asked for money. I could feel my ego judgment begin to think of excuses to avoid her. I quickly knew however, that was not what I was there to see. This was the holy Child of God masquerading in her story, as I was in mine. This was an opportunity to use the awareness that I want to accept as my belief. She immediately seemed to change as I saw her for who she is. Her frown became a smile that I knew had less to do with the money I had given her than the real gift that was given both of us. And I better understood what Jesus means when he tells us the Love of God is in us now waiting only an opportunity to be recognized.

My Mirror

If you hate anyone it must be yourself. There is no one you fear, except yourself. The world only mirrors what you think is true about you. But in fact, you neither hate nor fear yourself either. It is only the image of a self, living in your imagination. Forgive yourself for what was only done in your imagination and you will free the world of all the hate and fear that it has only dreamed of. And when the hate and fear have gone and only love remains, you can then accept that the world has never been "out there," but only an inner mirror of your dreaming self.

Understanding is the ego's substitute for trust.

Sacrifice

One of the most powerful blocks to the awareness we are loved unconditionally is the idea of sacrifice. Sacrifice arises solely from the belief we are guilty. It is our primary justification for pain and suffering. In the ego's upside-down perception, to sacrifice for someone is seen as a way to show your love for them. In truth, since it imposes a condition to loving it is an attack on love. Sacrifice is what the ego uses in place of forgiveness to "atone" for its guilt. When sacrifice in any form seems loving, remind yourself that this feeling began with guilt and can only separate you from the love you want.

Rather than trying to "train" your ego to be peaceful, say to your God Self, "Live my life for me that I may observe who I am."

When everyone is entitled to receive your love, love will come to you from everywhere.

One Mind

The Presence of love is recognized as we become aware that minds are joined. The unity of the one Mind is what gives love its function and its purpose. Recognize that when you re willing to forgive and join with the one you have judged you are offered the opportunity to experience what love is. What can come to you in these moments transcends this world entirely for you will witness the force that defines the eternal nature of God's Creation.

Where you are in your willingness to love determines your ability to recognize what is true.

It is an irreversible Law of God that you will be forever loved.

Time Or Eternity?

Time and eternity cannot both be real. You will decide which is true for you as you choose to judge or to forgive. One releases you from the story of the past, the other ensures that you will repeat it. The nature of love does not come and go. Who you are has not changed with time. And the Presence of eternal love is only found in the eternal now.

The holy instant is the length of time it takes to restore the memory of perfect peace and love to the mind of the holy Child of God.

All forms of lack are symptoms of the belief that we are disconnected from the Source of Love.

Choose For All

To remember you are one with all creation you must open your mind to this possibility. A good practice to help with this is to consciously begin to make choices that you intend to be for the benefit of the whole consciousness. As you do this intentionally and begin to feel the loving connection that results, you will recognize how natural this is. Continue and it soon will be apparent that every choice you have ever made has impacted the whole consciousness. Only if our separateness were real would it be possible to make choices for ourselves alone.

Knowing

Moving from not knowing to knowing seems to require much learning. There appears to be many things we do not know because we have denied that we are the Source of Knowing. It is the belief that we have sinned and lost the connection to This Source that has completely distorted our awareness; cut us off from our knowing. In truth, there is but one thing we need to learn – we cannot divide and make different what God created like Himself. Knowing this answers every question. Take a step to knowing today. Consider there is nothing wrong with you.

The Split Mind

Reality and illusion. The awareness of both is in our mind now. This seems to split our mind giving the impression that everything in our awareness has an opposite. The awareness that arises from each becomes a "world." Which world we see depends on which awareness we consider to be real. The world we now see comes from the belief in sin and guilt. This means it is a world of judgment and punishment, pain and suffering, attack and separation. But as surely as this world arises from the belief that we are guilty, there is another world that will replace it when we turn to the awareness, also now present but hidden, that nothing can change what God created like Himself.

Learning ends with real forgiveness for now you know that you are free to love

Who Is Sick?

The first step in healing is to determine "who" is sick. Regardless of what the pain may seem to be, remind yourself it is not you—the real you—that is sick. You are the changeless Child of God; the extension of all God Is. To believe that you could be sick is to imagine that God could be sick. The one who is sick is the character in the story you tell, the image of a self you have made that portrays you as a guilty person. Recognize this and what needs to be healed changes entirely. Now you realize it is only you who must decide if the healing is justified.

Where You Live

Everything that exists—all of creation—is an experience of thought that happens in the Mind of God, the only Mind that Is. This is where we are indivisibly joined. This is where we recognize we are when our belief is free of guilt. Ask to be shown this place to experience that freedom even for a moment. Feel the Love of God as it constantly embraces and sustains all that is here. Feel the recognition that this is where you live. Now capture this moment and ask your God Self to bring it to you when you are next tempted to judge a story where conflict and suffering seem so real.

To learn how to love, forgive what is not true. Only the belief in sin hides the awareness that God's Love, and yours, is always everywhere.

Consider this: If you had no reason to defend yourself from your brother, would he attack you? Recognizing the true answer to this would result in world peace.

Use Of forgiveness

Watch that you do not use forgiveness of guilt to offset the pain and misery that guilt causes. To forgive what is not real to avoid what you think is its real effect on you may free you momentarily from its effects, but will ultimately support your belief that your guilt is real and deserving to be feared. Remind yourself that you are created from love to extend love and what is being forgiven is your belief that there is something other than love that can affect you.

Lack

How many ways can the ego distract us from the recognition that all feelings of lack, be they of money, health or love, are really the belief that there is something lacking in us? When you have this feeling, remind yourself: The experience of lack in any form is only symbolic of our belief that we are deprived of our completeness, cut off from the rest of Creation. Everything we try to gain in the world is an attempt to overcome what we think is missing in us. In truth, the only thing missing is our memory of being connected to every other living thing. Recognizing this, it is obvious that "connecting" with one another is the only thing that will ever overcome any of our other feelings of lack.

Would you knowingly cling to something that brought you pain? If you judge guilt is real in anyone, the answer is yes.

Look For What Is Loving

Healing is not about fixing what is broken. Healing is being aware that you are created from perfect love for the purpose of extending perfect love and recognizing you cannot change what you are. But to remember what you are you must stop trying to be something else. Forgive the world and let it be a mirror for what is true about you. Look for what is loving and you will find love within yourself. Forgive what you have condemned and discover how the power of seeing differently will change your world.

Expect To Find Love

You must look for and expect to encounter love before you will find it. "Seeing" in the world is a mirror of our thoughts. What we see is as broad or as narrow as our perception will allow. We do not see things because they appear in the world. They appear in the world because the thought they portray first appeared in our mind. That is why finding love begins with our intention to find it. Forgiveness is what best establishes this intention. It removes the self-judgments we have used to separate us from love. The next time you feel unloved forgive someone that you have judged and discover where love is.

Condemn God?

The next time you feel compelled to condemn someone for what has happened in the world, ask yourself if you would condemn God for what your brother seems to have done. The world is a story we tell, a dream we have of happenings that have no meaning and no effect on anything outside the dream. As surely as God is not a part of our story, neither is the brother we have judged. What we judge is only a broken and distorted caricature of him and of our self. The one we think we judge is not there. But as long as we persist in judging him we will think that it is him and hold ourselves apart and miss the joy of loving him and feeling loved by God.

Being Happy

List all of the things your ego says you need to be happy.
Notice that the one thing they have in common is that they all
seem to require sacrifice or be extremely difficult to obtain.
Having a lovely relationship, a beautiful home or a healthy
body is not what causes us to be happy. Nothing in the world
is the cause of anything. It is always the effect. Our
happiness depends simply on not feeling the need to look
for something to fulfill us. It is important we remind ourselves
of this to keep our mind open to the Self within that is always
happy.

Awakening

During a conversation I had with a friend about Jesus life, he asked if I was aware, or had been told, if or when he had reached the moment of his awakening to the truth about himself. As he was asking the question I began to see the setting of the crucifixion. There were four crosses; one was empty. Many people were gathered at the site. Some were close, most were at a distance as if unsure about being seen there. It was an overcast but very still day. As I "watched" I was aware that he was floating in and out of physical consciousness, but his mind was fully at peace. It felt as if he wasn't really "there." I also was aware that I was anticipating that what I was going to "see" was a kind of flash of light and he would disappear. What I saw was his body become light that quickly filled my vision. It was the world that had disappeared. The symbolism was perfectly clear. What was real was unchanged. When he had awakened to the truth the thought of sin and a world of separateness that was not real had left his mind and the experience of it simply ceased to be. It was a vivid illustration of what he teaches.

Looking For Love?

If you would find the truth of the love and holiness within you, you must see past the unloving image you have come to believe is who we are. You cannot find it in the story you have made. The one you look for is not there. But we can learn to remember the truth of who we are by looking for it in our brother. Forgive him for deceiving himself and you have let go of your own deception. See him as he is right now and save yourself the need to redeem the image of smoke you have made to replace your Self. See him now free of his illusions and find the love and holiness that is already within you.

An Insight From Linda

Anytime you focus on differences, on what is right or wrong, no matter how good your intention seems to be, you are mentally stepping away from the Light of Love's Presence. In the same way, when you focus on the need to heal something, you are reinforcing the ego's belief that there is something wrong. Instead, focus on the perfection of the Light within yourself. Hold to the feeling that you, and all the world, are already healed. Focus only on what is real. Here, and only here, is where true happiness exists—and where happiness is, healing is as well.

Pivotal Experience

For some time now I have been using Brother's suggestions about consciously choosing to have a happy, peaceful and loving day as soon as I awaken in the mornings. My lesson is to find that as I choose for these I can trust my God Self to show me how to have them through guidance or correcting the choices I had made that would conflict with having them. It is a practice of learning that I can turn my day over to guidance and achieve my real goals.

About a week ago I read in ACIM a simple statement that had great implications for me that I have been pondering ever since. It was from chapter 30, section VI, paragraph 5: *"Forgiveness recognized as merited will heal."* Letting in the broader meaning of this statement has stayed with me. I could feel it having to do with my resistance to accepting that what I see in the world is not "real." There has always seemed to be another "corner" I needed to turn; another piece to add to what was missing.

This morning I awakened about 2 AM from a silly dream; not a "bad" one, just nonsensical. I thought then how much more I would prefer to have a happy dream and consciously chose to "be with" Brother, remembering our times together. I awakened again about dawn filled with a nearly euphoric sense of peace and happiness. The thought that filled my mind was: *Everything you have been looking for, you already have.*

As I lay there, only a little awake, the thought expanded. There is nothing more to do. You know the truth. Simply accept that moment I did know the truth. There was nothing missing in me. I was already healed and whole! And I was ecstatically happy. I also saw the real role that forgiveness plays for us. Forgiveness is the way I choose to be a witness to what is real, the way I practice "seeing differently;" the way I learn to recognize what is real as I let the experience of using it re-create my world.

I have heard all these words before, but now I felt their truth and they filled my mind with utter joy. Everything you ever looked for you already have. For that moment I was free of all ideas of sin and guilt and I could recognize that I was loved by everyone and there was no one I did not love completely. And in this feeling they were a part of me. It is this awareness of freely loving and being loved without any seeming "reason" or justification that connects us because it is true for everyone. Everyone feels exactly as I do. This is the meaning of "oneness." It is being joined with a force that is completely compelling simply because nobody wants anything else.

It is true. Nothing is wrong or bad, painful or lacking aside from the story we are telling. It is a movie made up about characters that exist only in the ego's perception. I can now feel another part of me that stands aside from the story, unchanged, unaffected in any way by whatever happens in it. I am free the moment I choose to let go of my story of being unloved. The words keep coming back. You are already healed. There is nothing broken or needing to be fixed. You cannot be unloved.

Cont'd

Pivotal Experience (Cont'd)

I can see now that forgiveness of all those things and people I had thought of as "broken" is the way I would learn to acknowledge that nothing real has happened; nothing has changed the essential me that has seemed lost in the story. Forgiveness truly removes the blocks to the awareness of Loves Presence.

What we must do is so very simple. We must just let go of what is not true. There is nothing broken that we need to fix. There is no world we need to save. There is just a thought that there is something wrong with us that we must acknowledge is not true, then let it go. The story we tell seems so real because it is our story. And it has the strength of our telling it a thousand times a day. It will seem to have a life of its own until we claim it by choosing to tell the forgiveness story instead.

Forgiveness seen as justified will heal. When I see something as healed and whole I will recognize what is true and truth will replace illusion in my world. Jesus does not ask that we tell someone how to become the Christ. He says simply, *"See the Christ in your brother."* Bring your recognition of his truth to our consciousness so that we all can share the awareness that we are healed because nothing has ever happened that can affect our reality. This is the, *"journey without distance from the place have never left."* Not judging what is not real will release us from all the effects of guilt. This is how we will bring the forgiven, real world into our consciousness.

Conscious Choosing

We reinforce our faith in what we believe will sustain us by the choices we make. Choosing to be defenseless means we have chosen to remove the purpose for attack from our own thoughts. There are no attack thoughts then in our mind to bring the experience of attack into our world. This makes no sense to the belief that we are separate and can victimize one another. Yet, once we begin to see how all our "scripts" are interwoven to reflect our common belief, nothing else does make sense.

Such A Simple Thing

Think for a moment of a world where there is no pain, no suffering or lack of any kind. There are no disasters, "natural" or otherwise. There are no thoughts that would interrupt a sense of constant joy. This is the world that exists in the mind that has forgiven it. Not partially or sometimes, but without regard to the form the world now associates with sin and fear. Such a seemingly simple thing. Know in your heart that what was created in the pure and loving Mind of God has never changed, cannot ever be changed. Just that. Believe that this is true and the mirror for this belief must rise to bless your sight.

True *forgiveness*

ACIM helps us to establish a basis for recognizing what is real and what is illusion. What is real arises from the intention of loving, of being one with all Creation. The experience that comes from thoughts of fear and divisiveness is not real because it does not support the reality of Creation being whole and undivided. It is upon this recognition that the use of true forgiveness rests. There is no basis for judging what is not real. There is no reason not to love what is real. Forgiveness allows us to remember the reality of what we have falsely judged, releasing our natural instinct to love again.

Only Our Thoughts Can Hurt Us

Pain and suffering are the penalties of guilt. They are also the price of ignorance for guilt is optional, it being self-imposed. Peace and joy and love are not the prize achieved for becoming a better person. They are the "option" when forgiveness replaces guilt as what we want. Only our thoughts can hurt us. Both attack and forgiveness may seem to focus on someone else, but their seeds are planted in our own mind, and it is there they both will first bear fruit.

Nothing "Outside" Ourselves

There is nothing in the world that can make us happy or sad, peaceful or afraid. For we have given all things we see there all the meaning that they have. "They," in fact could not exist without the purpose we have for them. And the purpose of the world we see, the thoughts we have, is to support the image of the ego self that we have made. To change our world, then, we must let go our concept of the self that it supports. To find a world that we can love we first must learn to forgive and love ourselves.

f

The Nature Of Love

When you find yourself wanting to express love to someone close to you, consciously expand your intention to include everyone, everywhere. Open yourself to the possibilities of where that intention will take you. Love has no measure, does not discriminate where to begin or end. Stay with this thought until you feel love returning to you. You will notice you cannot tell if it was "your" love or it had another "source," for love, to be love, must bring everything it touches together; it will be discovered wherever you choose to find it. Now, rest here a moment more and bask in the realization that every loving thought that has ever existed in the Mind of God – was meant for you.

When Love Replaces Fear?

We have made the world then given it the purpose to punish and imprison us, to justify our fears and teach us the danger of trusting love. In it we see our one consciousness divided into bodies with separate minds that cannot join, that suffer pain and die. Yet, We have made this world. Its only purpose is to serve us. We can change its purpose and the goal we have given it. It can become a "place" where love replaces fear and happiness abounds, when that is all we want for everyone we see.

When we forgive ourselves and our guilt is gone, we will see nothing in all the world we do not love.

Moment of Truth

Create a moment when everyone you see, all those you can think of, are filled with a loving glow. Their smiles beckon you to join them. There is no trace of conflict here for every thought, both yours and theirs, flow together in perfect harmony. There is nothing to be lost or gained for everyone is wholly loved. Hold this thought as what you want. This is not your imagination. It is a moment of truth and you have made it real by wanting it to be so.

Two Ways To See

There are two entirely different ways for us to think and see. Both are motivated by what we expect to find. One looks for what is wrong and finds a world made to meet its expectations. The other looks for a light it dimly remembers but cannot find with eyes that see the world guilt has made. But it persists, as it must do, for it cannot be satisfied with less than what is true. It looks for goodness and for love within itself then embraces all it sees with that vision, making everything like itself and part of what it is. Choose the Vision of the God Self and welcome Heaven into your mind.

To stay in the present moment, accept yourself now. When you accept yourself as innocent and complete in this moment there is nothing in the past to judge and nothing for you to become in the future. You are now free from the need for time.

What Comes First?

What comes first, the way someone treats you, or your expectation of it. We cannot be too often reminded that our primary challenge in changing our experience in the world is to change what we are looking for, what we expect to find. Is it possible to find only love in the world I now see? Can I trust what someone would do if I just loved them? If you feel it is worth the "risk" to find out, say to your God Self, "I am willing today not to be afraid of love. Help me." Then know that with this intention you have altered the course of the world.

Know All Things As They Are

Amidst all of our uncertainties and challenges our daily prayer need only be, "Let me know all things exactly as they are." We can free ourselves from the stress and fear of yet another variation of what will satisfy the ego's needs by remembering that finding peace and happiness, being free of lack and pain, does not come from our efforts for "self improvement." These are attacks on what God has created whole and perfect. All that we must change is the mistaken idea that there is something about us that we must change.

When we try to elevate or lower a brother to a different, spiritual status, please remember, if there was someone who could awaken at a different "time" than you, it would prove that dreams are real and separateness is true.

Helping Others

When someone does not see the truth of who they are, how often have you wondered what you should do to help? In truth, we need only find and accept the truth of who we are. When others are ready to "see," that awareness is shared. Linear, or sequential time, becomes irrelevant, for In that moment, time and space are set aside and the vision you hold will register wherever and whenever it is needed.

The Two-Way Mirror

The ego's world is like a two-way mirror. It exactly reflects from the inside – out all of its beliefs of what it perceives is wrong with it. It then sees these beliefs from the other side— the outside—as though its "sins" belonged to the world and it now must suffer their effects. Seeing like this, it then believes it is the victim of the world that it has made. It still suffers the payment guilt demands but at the hand of an avenging world and not its own. Is this insane, or what?

Everyone Wants To Be Loved

There is no one who does not want to be happy and at peace; no one who does not want to be loved. Yet, the world we now see seems to be becoming progressively more chaotic. This is not because we are "regressing," but because the thoughts that are expressing our fear of joining are resisting our willingness to join. Each time one of us chooses to be loving where we have previously condemned, peace and happiness is more easily chosen by everyone.

Guilt

Guilt is to our belief like wearing colored glassed is to our sight—everything you see is colored by it. It is our thoughts that make the world and the purpose of them now supports all that we expect from guilt. You can't learn how to cope with guilt. There is no amount of sacrificing that will atone for it. If it is part of your belief it will underlie all that motivates you. You will, in short, feel inclined to judge anyone for any reason at all.

The only way to deal with guilt is to realize that its cause, "sin," is impossible because it is not the Will of God Whose creation must be like Himself. Then let it go because it does not support what is true about you. Let it go by not making choices that judge what others do. Teaching that sin is not true is the primary function of the God Self, which we learn through the practice of forgiveness.

Holding and maintaining this awareness in response to all that the ego's perception demands is true, is our only real function in the world. What we experience then through the practice of forgiveness is what it is like to feel the power of love when it is free of the influence of guilt. Bringing this awareness to our consciousness is what will then make our world a peaceful and loving experience.

The Will Of God

There is a simple way to recognize the Will of God: It always begins with loving and everything it expresses is received with love. And as we recognize that Love expresses the Will of God we need only to remember to set our intention to be loving to know that our will and the Will of God is one.

Sameness Or Differences?

What makes someone different from you? Is it how they look, the way they think or what they want? Since all bodies are basically the same and we share the same perception and want exactly the same thing, it must be something else. Differences actually only exist in our desire to be separate; to have someone "else" to blame for what we feel guilty of. Discovering that this is true is the role of forgiveness. When we have forgiven the world and discover the loving presence of each brother, "sameness" is what we will value most.

Willingness To Love

Is there something about the world that could justify my not loving it? Is there something about the world that I have not made? When I can finally answer "no" to both of these I will know why I can only feel loved to the extent that I am willing to love.

Becoming Fearless

To free ourselves from fear we must remember that fear is only possible when love seems missing. Yet where is there for love to go when it is the foundation of who we are? When fear arises then, no matter what seems to be its cause, know it is your call for love and ask for the opportunity to love another as you wish to be loved.

f

We Are Not At Home Among Our Fearful Thoughts

We are not at home among our thoughts that look for fault, anticipate pain and move us in isolation from one another. We seem at times to wander among an ever-shifting stream of fearful, contradicting thoughts that lead nowhere. We wonder why peace seems so elusive, joy so quickly lost. The simple truth is our mind is filled with chaos because we have condemned ourselves. We judge everything we see because we have condemned the one who sees it. We long to be free of the thoughts that plague us. We look for distraction in the things we do. We may even try surrendering our thoughts to our God Self. But until we have forgiven the only one we ever have really judged, our perception of guilt must persist, and our thoughts will all validate that it is true. Take your belief to your God Self with the intention of surrendering not only your thoughts, but also the belief from which they arise. Forgive yourself and watch your thoughts support a forgiven world.

Finding God

The purpose of pretending to be different and separate from our brothers is to have others we can pretend to judge for what we secretly believe to be *our* "sins." The purpose of forgiveness is to discover there is no sin. The purpose of the God Self is to show us how to use forgiveness to change the purpose of the world and find God in all the places we had thought there was something else to find. Then, for just an instant let go all your judgments and in that quiet moment know that God has found you.

The Miracle Of Real *forgiveness*

The miracle of real forgiveness is discovering the freedom that comes with accepting that part of your Self you had previously condemned. It is learning that releasing a brother from "his" guilt is the same as releasing you from yours. We are part of a single consciousness, interconnected in our common story about sin and separation. Believing we can awaken alone is like imagining one thought in our mind could change while the others remained as they were.

Where will you find a sinless world? The same place you found the one dedicated to hate and blame and guilt— in your "split" mind. Which you accept as real depends on what you think is true about yourself. Forgive yourself and set the world free!

Changing Our Mind

God's Will for us is perfect happiness. It is for peace beyond anything the ego's perception can imagine. He has placed the Voice for Truth within our mind for us to hear and use to guide us in the choices that we make. But it is we who must make the choices in order to claim the benefits that they can bring. Choose peace in the presence of fear and peace becomes our reality. Choose to love when love seems to have lost its way and we have become the presence of love. Let the Voice for God choose through us and we have ended the separation we have imagined to exist there.

Thought Of The Day

Think for a moment what it would be like to go about your day with your mind filled only with happy and loving thoughts. Everyone you meet has a smile and a glow of happiness about them. There is no sickness, no hunger, no conflict or lack; no striving, no blame, no expectations, no time and no death. Peace has replaced fear everywhere. There is no word to describe hate for all the reasons not to love are gone. This is our mind without the thought of sin. This is our world when there is no guilt to judge.

Changing Your World

We have no real concept of the power of our mind to create our world or to heal our bodies because we use it now to make stories about what happens *to us* and what is wrong with us. Learning to use it for a different purpose requires that we begin to think outside the "guilt box"; to assume that the best and not the worst is true. For five minutes take the image of everyone who crosses your mind to the Presence of your God Self and ask to see only what is true about them. What you see thereafter in the world will never be the same.

You cannot Decide "Selectively" Who to Love

When you think of yourself as guilty and separate, believing that your concerns and desires are different from others, you cannot interact or join with anyone, even those you might think you want to be close to. The ego does seem to be able to decide who it will accept and those it must reject, but in truth this has more to do with perception and judging than with loving. The ego's perception demands selectively choosing who is worth loving and who must fall short of your approval. But judgment and real loving are completely incompatible. If love is real it must embrace everything it touches. Judgment comes from the belief that there is something wrong with you. This then becomes the way you see all the world, for you see everything through the same perception that you see yourself. In this one thing is the ego perfectly consistent. Knowing this it then becomes apparent that every judgment made condemns *everything* in your perception, even those things or people you might think you like. Remember too each time you refuse to accept your story of guilt and fear as being true, your forgiveness frees you to see another world where judgment does not exist. Here, without the judgment of yourself, you are free to join, free to know the joy that comes with remembering how to love indiscriminately!

Guilt Or Innocence

There are two entirely different ways for us to think and so to see. Both are motivated by what we expect to find. One looks for what is wrong because it sees through a veil of guilt and finds a world made to meet its expectations. The other looks for a Light it dimly remembers but cannot find with eyes that see the world guilt has made. But it persists, as it must do, for it cannot be satisfied with less than what is true. It looks for goodness and for love within itself then embraces all it sees with that loving vision, making everything like itself and part of what it is. Do this and discover that you are the bringer of the Light, the holder of the Truth. Yours are the choices that release our consciousness from hatred and from fear.

You are free when you are without the need to judge; when there is no reason not to love. Being without the need to judge comes with the recognition there is nothing wrong with you, no reason for you not to be loved. It is here we finally begin to realize what freedom really means.

The Power Of Our Thoughts

A Dialogue with Jesus:

"While focusing on the physical world, it is difficult for you to be aware of the impact of your thinking. You are accustomed to presuming things there have a physical cause. This is why your role of holding an inner vision of a forgiven world is so significant, for that is where changes in the awareness of the ego's consciousness occur. But as you do this please remember, it is the Holy Spirit that uses your intention for this vision in circumstances and in ways you cannot see."

"Where" Are We?

When we think about giving up this world the first thing that comes to mind is letting go of those we love here. We have forgotten it is not they we would be giving up, but only our misperception of them. Neither they nor we are in our story of the world. What we see here are the characters in our story. Consider how much greater our love for them will be when we see who they really are. How satisfying it is to know there is no pain for them to suffer and no death to separate us. And where in our one Mind could we go and not be joined with what is part of us?

f

A Message from brother

Brother tells us we need to learn to identify ourselves as spirit, not bodies; as the tellers of our story not the character in it – as spirit not form. I have been trying to do this for some time – unsuccessfully. There is nothing familiar to identify. With Linda and our friend Josh, I ask yet again:

Brother sez:

"It is the need to be separate that drives the need to have an identity. Concurrently you are beginning to feel what it is like to explore the many facets of loving. This exploration leads to an entirely different place in your awareness from which to identify yourself as well as a different purpose for doing so. In the ego' awareness identifying anything sets it apart and gives it a limitation. Love knows no boundaries as your Self knows none either. You are the experience of God Loving, as is all He Created. As this identification becomes accepted your need for other false identities will fall away.

I don't mean to further confuse you, but when I say you are the experience of God Loving, I could also say you are the intelligence of God becoming manifest, for in truth Love and intelligence are the same. Making this connection will be helpful for you to find fewer reasons, fewer temptations to distinguish yourself from God."

We are all "hitch hikers" on the highway to Love. Pull over when you see brother or sister asking for a lift and be reminded we are all going to the same place.

Pretend that sin is a fairytale; it happens in our stories but is too obviously impossible to be true. It is not a creation of God and would deny His Will for perfect happiness. See the world that sin has made as an opportunity to deny the denial of Love and live as though Love was the only thing you wanted to give or to even see. Literally, see yourself as the Presence of God Loving. Open your Mind to the infinite possibilities of God Loving. Use

forgiveness

to abandon separateness and become the
DOORWAY TO LOVE AND TO PEACE.

And above all, remember
We but imagine a journey from a place
We have never left.

Made in the USA
Middletown, DE
02 July 2020